Revolutionary
BERGEN COUNTY

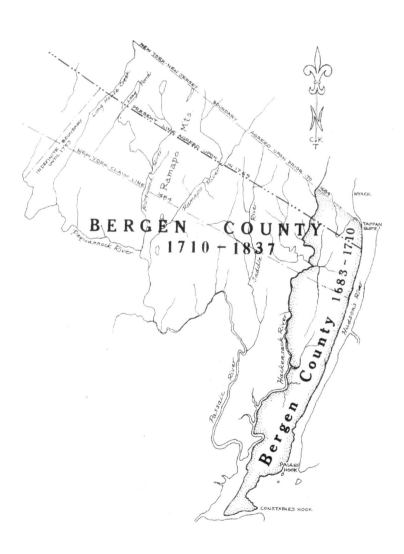

NEW YORK-NEW JERSEY

BOUNDARY

Long House Creek

PRESENT LINE AGREED UPON IN 1769

AGREED UPON PRIOR TO

Ramapo Mts.

INDEFINITE BOUNDARY UNTIL 1773

NEW YORK CLAIM LINE 1684

Rockpond River

Ramapo River

River

1684

NYACK

TAPPAN SLOTE

BERGEN COUNTY
1710 – 1837

Pequannock River

Saddle

Hudson's River

River

Bergen County 1683 – 1710

Passaic River

Hackensack River

Hudson's River

PAULUS HOOK

CONSTABLES HOOK

Old photo postcard showing Tice/Tise Tavern in Jersey City (part of Bergen County during the Revolutionary War). It was called the Eagle Tavern when Washington and Lafayette met there during the Revolutionary War. *From the collection of Barbara Marchant.*

Revolutionary BERGEN COUNTY

THE ROAD TO INDEPENDENCE

EDITED BY BARBARA Z. MARCHANT

THE
History
PRESS

Published by The History Press
Charleston, SC 29403
www.historypress.net

Front cover:
American Troops Retreating, Liberty Pole. *Illustration by permission of Gray's Watercolors,*
grayswatercolors@rcn.com.
Fife. *Courtesy of the Schoolhouse Museum, Ridgewood, NJ. Ira Lieblich, photographer.*

Back cover:
British Scaling the Palisades II. *Illustration by permission of Gray's Watercolors, grayswatercolors@*
rcn.com.
British-made pistol. *Courtesy of the Schoolhouse Museum, Ridgewood, NJ. Ira Lieblich, photographer.*

Page 1
Bergen County map showing county lines from 1683 to 1837.
Courtesy of the Bergen County Historical Society.

First published 2009

Manufactured in the United States

ISBN 978.1.59629.748.7

Library of Congress CIP data applied for.

Contents

CONTENTS

Foreword

REVOLUTIONARY BERGEN COUNTY

M any readers will be surprised to learn that Bergen County, in northeastern New Jersey, stood in the eye of the Revolutionary storm. After the war broke out in 1775 and the British were expelled from Boston less than a year later, they set their sights on the mouth of the Hudson River as the greatest strategic prize on the American continent. By capturing New York City and sending a second British force down from Canada, the British expected to control the Hudson, physically divide the American colonies—New England from the Mid-Atlantic and the South—and crush the rebellion. Bergen County, extending along the western shore of the Hudson River across from Manhattan and Lower Westchester County, was the scene of Washington's headlong retreat with Lord Cornwallis at his heels, after the British drove the Continental army out of New York in November 1776 and settled in for a seven-year occupation.

The following year, when British commander in chief General William Howe decided to add the American capital, Philadelphia, to his laurels, New Jersey as a whole truly became the crossroads of the American Revolution: caught between Philadelphia to the west and New York City to the east, traversed and raided by the armies of both sides, New Jersey by war's end was the site of 238 battles—more than any other state. With Washington's troops holed up in the mountains of northern and central New Jersey, monitoring the route to Philadelphia and ambushing British foraging parties, Bergen County was wedged even more tightly between the two contending armies. Nominally a "neutral zone" acting as a buffer between the British and Americans, the county was intensely polarized, with Whig and Tory neighbors locked in a brutal civil war. Finally, in 1781, Bergen County became a key part of the route to American victory, where Washington and his French allies feigned an attack on New York on their way to trap Cornwallis at Yorktown.

The richly detailed essays in this collection bring Revolutionary Bergen County to life, revealing the upheaval and suffering endured by individuals caught between opposing armies and torn by conflicting allegiances to family, church, community and country. Exploring the perspectives of Loyalists and Patriots at every level of the struggle from the frontlines to the homefront, the collection also places us firmly in the landscape of Bergen County, identifying roadways, historic markers and sites of interest—some still standing, and some that have vanished without a trace. The essays reveal the human drama behind the historic structures and documents: the ordeal of the road to independence. These little-known stories add a new dimension to our understanding of the nation's founding, while offering valuable lessons for America's future leaders.

Barnet Schecter

Author, *The Battle for New York: The City at the Heart of the American Revolution*

ACKNOWLEDGMENTS

This book would not have been possible without the help of so many people to whom I shall be forever grateful:

The contributing authors are the top guns of Bergen County's Revolutionary War history. Thank you, all!

Special mention to Todd Braisted and Kevin Wright, past presidents of the Bergen County Historical Society; to Firth Fabend, Fellow of the New Netherland Project and of the Holland Society; and to John U. Rees. All are published writers many times over and generously took the time to contribute to this book while working on their other projects. I am so very grateful.

The members of the Bergen County Historical Society, the Bergen County Division of Cultural and Historic Affairs, Crossroads of the American Revolution Association and other historical commissions and societies in the county all gave their encouragement to this project. Kevin Tremble, Crossroads of the American Revolution Association president and owner of Tech Repro, gave guidance on the images and essays to be included. Kevin also introduced me to Pat Finn and Jim Wright, who wrote the piece on John Fell. A big thank-you goes to the wonderful Robert Gerber of Tech Repro who scanned all the images that you see in this book.

I am indebted to The History Press and their terrific editors: my commissioning editor, Saunders Robinson, and my copy editor, Deborah Carver. They were both supportive and positive from beginning to end.

My heartfelt gratitude goes to my friends and Leonia's sweethearts, Martha Lieblich, who is on the board of the Crossroads of the American Revolution Association, and her husband, fellow Brooklynite Ira Lieblich, for spending hours driving around Bergen County taking many of the photographs of the historic markers and artifacts that are in this book. I also thank them for feeding me throughout the month of July 2009 (well, all of the other months, too) while I was editing and indexing this book.

Mona and Michael Rubin, dear friends, also supported me with food and sage advice.

A big thank-you goes to friend William Neumann, who is also a contributor to this book. Billy, a professional photographer, looked over the images and gave his fabulous advice as to what would be best for the book.

Thanks and hugs go to new grandparents Darryl and Patricia Whitter for always looking out for Chez Marchant and me.

Many thanks to Steven Weigl, director of the Bergen County Historical Society research library, and to his two volunteer worker bees, Averal Genton and Dee Cobianchi. Barbara Flurchick and Rosann Pellegrino gave their time and history smarts, and I am so happy to serve on the BCHS board with them. Jeannette Pook of the First Reformed Church ("Church on the Green") in Hackensack assisted Martha and Ira Lieblich with Brigadier General Enoch Poor's grave site information.

Special thanks to the historical reenactment groups, particularly the Brigade of the American Revolution (BAR); Outwater's Militia; the Continental Line; and In Good Company, an eighteenth-century dance group. There would be quite a gap in our knowledge if these wonderful people did not give so much of their time to bring the history that they cherish into our lives.

A very special thank-you goes to Toren Shahar, my Apple computer expert and son of my dearest friend, Lauri Shahar. Toren helped when my Mac's hard drive started to crash and, although he lives in Los Angeles, was able to share my laptop screen and help me save all of my work before I overdosed on milk chocolate bars.

I would like to thank my wonderful friends for all of their love and support while I was editing: Lauri (aka Wayward) Shahar, Martha Lieblich, Mona Rubin, Liz Horvitz, Carol Karels and Carol Rozman, Nancy Terhune, Bobbi Warden, Erika Bacchia, Jo Radcliffe, Moira Palandri and my friends from Table 5. The title of this book included the generous efforts of Carol K., Mona and Martha.

A very big thank-you to my dear friend, the terrific Carol Karels, the editor of *The Revolutionary War in Bergen County: The Times that Tried Men's Souls*, for her encouragement and advice on editing.

My heart-felt gratitude to another dear friend, the fabulous Nancy Terhune, for her suggestion of contributors to this book and her assistance in copy editing and proofreading.

Thanks go to my American family for their love: my incredible sister, Diane; brother-in-law, Tom; my brothers, Kevin and Keith; sister-in-law, Leeann; my dad, Bill; my nieces, Kelly, Ashley, Courtney, Kimberly and Kaylee; and my nephew, Keith. Finally, because of my much-missed husband, Peter, I have another family in England who give me support. I am thankful every day for having had Peter in my life, but I still have Ann, Billy, John, Freddie, Mike, Sue, Irene and Geoff. Cheers!

If I have neglected to thank anyone, I apologize for the oversight. Every contribution, great or small, helped make this book what it is.

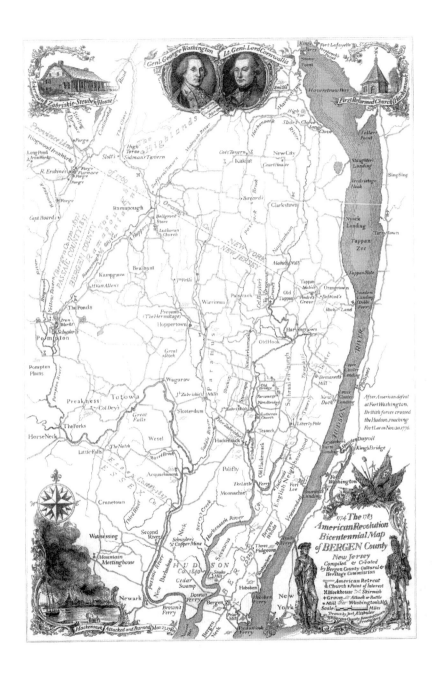

The American Revolution Bicentennial Map of Bergen County. *Courtesy of the Bergen County Division of Cultural and Historic Affairs.*

INTRODUCTION

After *The Revolutionary War in Bergen County: The Times that Tried Men's Souls* had been out for a short while, folks started asking us—the authors— when the "next Rev War book" would arrive. Having tasted the richness and drama of the county's Revolutionary history, people wanted more. And those who had contributed essays to that book knew that there remained many fascinating stories of riveting events, intriguing people and interesting places that deserved their moments in the sun. This book is a continuation of, not a sequel to, *The Revolutionary War in Bergen County: The Times that Tried Men's Souls* (or as we sometimes call it, *RW1*), and it is every bit as remarkable.

This book, like the first, is an eclectic mix of stories told from different perspectives: the British, the Hessians, the Loyalists, the Continentals, the Patriot militias and the civilian residents of the county who endured over seven years of wartime strife. You'll see some of the same authors who wrote in *RW1* here, but there are new contributors, too.

One wonderful addition to this book is the foreword written by Barnet Schecter, author of my favorite book on the Revolutionary War, *The Battle for New York: The City at the Heart of the American Revolution.* I had met Barnet at various history-related events over the years. At an event in Fort Greene Park, Brooklyn, in August 2008, I asked if he might be willing to write the foreword to a book I would be editing about the Revolution in Bergen County. To my amazement and delight, he said that he would. I cannot express how much I appreciate his taking the time to read the entire book and write such a striking foreword.

My quest to find an interesting cover image had a happy ending. Like Carol Karels, editor of *The Revolutionary War in Bergen County: The*

Times that Tried Men's Souls, I looked for an image that hadn't been overused. In the course of combing through the research library of the Bergen County Historical Society (BCHS), library director and fellow BCHS trustee Steven Weigl helped me locate many Revolutionary War images. We found some black-and-white scenes painted by a local artist, Davis Gray. I returned home, searched the Internet and—lo and behold!—I found the Gray's Watercolors website. I made contact with the organization and was able to obtain permission from Wilda McConaughy of Gray's Watercolors to use some of Davis Gray's terrific paintings for this book.

Though proudly from historic Brooklyn, I never really appreciated the history of the New Jersey/New York area until I had lived in Bergen County for a couple of years. After my late husband Peter and I had moved to Leonia, I joined the newly formed Leonia Historic Preservation Commission in late 1991. I felt that this was a good time to learn some local New Jersey history despite my view that history happened primarily in other places in the United States and not where I lived. When I was growing up in Brooklyn, I had no clue that George Washington had been there. Any book that even mentioned Washington's connection with New York always mentioned Long Island, so I assumed Washington was somewhere out in Nassau County, not in Kings County, Brooklyn!

Once I started learning about the incredible events that occurred both in New Jersey and New York City, there was no stopping my desire to study our rich, local history. Peter was somewhat less awestruck because he had grown up in southeast England near Roman ruins, but he did share my new enthusiasm for the history here. We increasingly appreciated what had occurred here during the Revolutionary War. I joined more organizations involved with local history: the Brooklyn Historical Society, Ridgewood [NJ] Historical Society, Bergen County Historical Society and the Fort Greene Park Conservancy Prison Ship Martyrs' Memorial Centennial Committee. One of the most exciting events in my history life was when I was able to contribute to *The Revolutionary War in Bergen County: The Times that Tried Men's Souls*, and now I am thrilled to be the editor of *Revolutionary Bergen County: The Road to Independence*.

As with the first Rev War book, all proceeds from retail sales will go to the Bergen County Historical Society, a nonprofit volunteer organization whose museum collections will, we all hope, soon be on display at a new visitor center at Historic New Bridge Landing. Please consider making a donation to the BCHS so it may continue to keep history alive with its educational talks, monthly events and a new visitor center. Online donations can be made at www.bergencountyhistory.org. Many thanks for your support!

Barbara Z. Marchant
Leonia, New Jersey
September 2009

————•————

Barbara Z. Marchant is a trustee of both the Bergen County Historical Society and the Ridgewood Historical Society, an active member of the Leonia Historical Preservation Commission, a member in 2008 of the Fort Greene (Brooklyn, New York) Park Conservancy Prison Ship Martyrs' Memorial Centennial Committee, a member of the Zoning Board of Adjustment in the Borough of Leonia and a former member of the Leonia Environmental Commission. Marchant has always had an interest in military history and grew up near the site of the first battle of the American Revolution in Brooklyn. She has also extensively researched two other major historical events during her time overseas: the Boxer Rebellion and the 1944 Normandy Invasion. She contributed two pieces—"The Retreat to Victory" and "General Charles Lee: A Disobedient Servant"—to The Revolutionary War in Bergen County: The Times that Tried Men's Souls.

Major Robert Timpany

Schoolmaster and Soldier

Todd W. Braisted

Those who educate a nation's youth in the ways of mathematics, English or science seldom get the chance to lead those same pupils on the field of battle, but such was the case of a Bergen County schoolmaster named Robert Timpany.

Robert Timpany was born on Christmas Day 1742 in Newtonards, County Down, Ireland, the son of Robert and Elizabeth Timpany of that place. The young Robert received his education at the University of Glasgow, Scotland. Immigrating to Philadelphia in 1760, he became a teacher there but eventually removed to Hackensack in Bergen County, New Jersey.

The exact location of Timpany's schoolhouse is not definitively known, but evidence suggests it was at New Bridge, on the east side of the Hackensack River, near the farm of Abraham Van Buskirk. Across the river would have been John Zabriskie, lieutenant colonel in the militia and, like Van Buskirk, politically loyal to the British government and King George the Third. Unlike Zabriskie and Van Buskirk (who was appointed surgeon to the Bergen County Militia in 1776), Timpany does not appear to have had any military appointment heading into the conflict. That would change.

While British troops chased Washington's army out of Manhattan and into Westchester, Lieutenant General Hugh Earl Percy informed his superior, Sir William Howe, in October that he had been contacted by a "Dr. Buskirk Chairman of the Committee in Bergen County" advising him that if the Crown forces entered the county "he has a thousand men ready with which he could join them." While the numbers were exaggerated, the British indeed received a warm welcome from hundreds of Loyalists

The Fourth Battalion, New Jersey Volunteers, fire a volley during the events of the 225th anniversary of Yorktown. *Courtesy of Mary Keller.*

when Lord Cornwallis and his five thousand men occupied the county the following month.

Abraham Van Buskirk had received a warrant from Cortland Skinner, the last attorney general under the Crown in New Jersey, empowering him to raise a battalion for His Majesty's service. Skinner would command the entire corps, known as the New Jersey Volunteers, while Van Buskirk would command the Fourth Battalion thereof. Each battalion was to consist of ten companies, with three officers per company, who would receive their commissions based on the number of men each raised.

Robert Timpany was in an excellent position to raise men for the service. After years of having Bergen County's youth under his tutelage, he had the advantages of being well known and respected in the Hackensack Township area, qualities well suited to raise men. Timpany and his two other would-be officers, Martin Ryerson and James Cole, quickly raised no fewer than sixty-five men from well-known families in the county: Christie, Ruttan, Post, Vandenburgh, Nix, Ramsey, Ackerman, Ackerson, etc. For their success, the three Loyalist gentlemen received their commissions to serve under Van Buskirk: Timpany as second major, Ryerson as lieutenant and Cole as ensign. Major Timpany's commission was dated November 18, 1776, possibly indicating that he had joined the British shortly before their entering the county.

Even while the battalion was still being organized and recruits assembled, Major Timpany joined in their first excursion. From Hackensack and New Bridge, a party was sent off to Tappan, the closest Rebel outpost, with an intention of surprising the post. The *New-York Gazette and the Weekly Mercury* printed the story afterward:

> *On Friday the 6th Instant, upon Information being given to Col. M'Donald (of the 71st Regiment) that a Party of the Rebels were at Tapan, in the Jersies, he immediately detached Capt. Skelly (also 71st Regt.) with his Company, who were posted at the New–Bridge in Hackinsack, to dislodge them. A Party of New–Jersey Volunteers, under the Command of Col. Abraham Van Buskirk, and Major Timpany, both of whom have ever been distinguished for their loyal Attachment to the King and Constitution, joined with Capt. Skelly in this Expedition. They advanced to Tapan, drove off the Rebels, and disarmed the suspected Inhabitants. The New–Jersey Volunteers hearing, that a Party of Rebel Officers were lodged at a little Distance from Tapan, immediately set out in Quest of them, and took one Rebel Capt., and two Lt.s, Prisoners.*

One of the captured officers was Lieutenant Aaron Stratton of the Sixteenth Continental Regiment, a Massachusetts unit. He would remain a prisoner on parole on Long Island until finally exchanged in January 1781.

The British reversals at Trenton and Princeton shortly thereafter led to a consolidation of outposts throughout the state. Bergen County, with the exceptions of Paulus Hook (part of present-day Jersey City) and Bergen Point (modern Bayonne), was evacuated. Major Timpany, along with the rest of the battalion, was relocated to Decker's Ferry on Staten Island, across from Bergen Point. The Loyalist Volunteers were not long at their new post when on February 27, 1777, Major Timpany again was called into action, as reported in the press: "On Thursday last, Major Tympany crossed from Staten Island to Elizabeth Town, with about 60 men, where he was attacked by a body of the rebels, two or three of whom were killed on the spot, and four or five taken prisoners. The Major returned safe, without having a man hurt, and brought with him ten head of cattle." An official return from 1780 showing captures made by the battalion until that point listed four prisoners taken at Rahway in March 1777 by Major Timpany, which was possibly the raid described above.

Duty on Staten Island proved eventful, particularly in providing security for both the inhabitants and the forces garrisoned there. On March 14, 1777, another opportunity presented itself for the major, making its way into the newspapers: "Last Friday Morning a Party of the Rebels came down on the Jersey Shore, and fired on some Boats that were taken in Forage at New-Blazing-Star, Staten-Island, on which Major Timpaney, of the Bergen Volunteers, crossed the River with about 40 Men, drove the Rebels above three Miles from the Water Side, and brought off ten Head of Cattle and about thirty Sheep, without the Loss of a Man."

The garrisoned battalion on Staten Island did not translate to safety and security for Bergen County's Whig inhabitants. Two raids in rapid succession that April brought that home. Twenty-five men under Captain Peter Ruttan captured John Fell at his home north of Hopperstown on April 23, 1777. Just three days later Brigadier General George Clinton was informed that "a party of the new levies under Coll. [Joseph] Barton, Leut't Coll. [Robert] Drummond & Major Timpany, said to consist of about two hundred, a little after sun rise this morning, surprised took & carried off Capt. W[ynan]t Van Zandt and three others from Garrit Hopper's neighbourhood[,] they also took twelve guns, five or six horses, a wagon, and a chest & Cask of goods from Hopper's the goods said to belong to P. Curtenus. They attempted several other of the neighbours, who either run off, or concealed themselves & escaped."

The remainder of the spring and into summer of 1777 saw a continuance of raids and counter-raids to and from Staten Island. Most involved parts of a total of six battalions of New Jersey Volunteers stationed on the island pitted against different units of New Jersey Militia. That equation changed on the steamy morning of August 22, 1777, when Major General John Sullivan led a force of two thousand Continental troops in three divisions onto the island in the hopes of crushing the Loyalist troops. Success initially attended the Continentals, as they took about 125 prisoners, primarily from the First and Fifth Battalions, New Jersey Volunteers, including their commanders. The troops going against the Fourth Battalion and Major Timpany were not so fortunate, however, as their guide deliberately brought them to Decker's Ferry in a manner that would alert the Loyalist garrison there, which prepared to receive them. Declining to attack, the Loyalists were free to pursue the retreating Continentals. The battalion, personally led by Brigadier General Cortland Skinner, marched to support the other parts of the corps scattered over the island. Major Timpany would play a most prominent role in the actions that followed:

Upon the Approach of the regular Troops the Rebels instantly marched off with all Speed. In the mean Time Brigadier General Skinner had collected those of his Corps that had been dislodged from their Stations, and detached Major Tympany with 25 Men to gain Information of the Route that the Enemy had taken. The Major came up with a Number of them at the House of Dr. Parker, which they were plundering. He attacked them immediately, killed several, and took the rest Prisoners; among the killed was Mr. Smallwood's Brigade Major.

The latter might be a reference to Captain James Heron of Congress's Own Regiment. The incident and the circumstances that led to it are described in wonderful detail by Captain Enoch Anderson of the Delaware Continental Regiment:

My line of march brought me near to a large brick house. Here I found some of the British. But a few only of them turned out—got round a haystack—fired one gun and then run. I drew up my men on the pavement and entered the house. An old female was there and no more. I soon found this was a Col.'s quarters, with his officers. She told me I had come so quickly upon them that they had run half-naked out of the house. I found the house full of lawful plunder. I went out to my soldiers and told them there was plenty of fair plunder inside. Go in, all of you, I said, I will stay here, but when you hear me beat the drum come out in a moment. I waited a due time and then beat the drum. They came out—each one having something.

As I was ready to march [Captain] Herron came with his party for plunder, and in the house he and all his soldiers went. He wanted me to wait, but I found the army gone and I told him I would not. At this moment a runner [arrived] to tell me and Herron to come on directly—that the enemy had landed troops from Long Island and would waylay us at the Red [Parker] House...I hallooed to Herron, who was in the upper story throwing out hats, &c., but he said he would not move until he and his soldiers were loaded with plunder!

I marched on, and I had not gone three hundred yards from the house when I was met by Colonel [John Hawkins] Stone at full

British-made pistol. *Courtesy of the Schoolhouse Museum, Ridgewood, New Jersey. Photograph courtesy Ira Lieblich.*

gallop. Run, run, says he, it's no disgrace. I passed the Red House by a short cut through a meadow filled with bushes—my men in single files and marched on with a double quick step. I had not gone more than a quarter of a mile, when a battle took place in my rear. This was Herron marching by the Red House. He was attacked here by the British—had eighteen killed and wounded and all the rest were taken prisoners—plunder and all.

Captain Heron was severely wounded by Timpany's men, but not killed. He was among 258 prisoners, including 22 officers, taken by the Loyalists and British that day. After the affair at the Parker House, the corps continued on to attack the remainder of the Continentals on their retreat, for which they received the thanks for the "Resolution & Conduct shown by Coll. Buskirk with the Spiritted behaviour of the Officers & Soldiers under his Command, in the Attack of the Rebel boats." The press reported, "Colonel Buskirk's Corps, merit the highest Praise for their ready Obedience to General [John] Campbell's Orders, and for their manly and brave efforts to annoy the Enemy."

Sir Henry Clinton, commanding the forces in the New York District while Sir William Howe was engaged in the Philadelphia Campaign, had Bergen County on his mind shortly after Sullivan's raid on Staten Island. From September 12 to 16, up to 3,500 British, German and Provincial troops, including 300 New Jersey Volunteers, foraged the county, rounding up cattle and buying or taking produce from the farmers. Aside from a spirited skirmish at Second River, described by Sir Henry himself:

> *At Day break the Rebels appeared in some Force, and about Noon they had three pieces of Cannon in Battery on their side of the Ravine. I went over to observe them, and had every reason to suppose, from their Cloathing and Artillery, that they were reinforced by what is called Continental Troops. To try their Countenance, and give an Opportunity to the Provincials, I ordered Buskirk's Battalion to March through a Corn Field, with an intention of taking in Flank a Body of the Rebels posted behind a Stone Wall, and which it would have been difficult to have removed by a Front Attack. The Regiment Marched with great Spirit, and their March, and some little movement to favour it, obliged the Rebels to quit without a Shot.*

It is not known whether Major Timpany was part of this expedition, but it is clear his schoolhouse figured in it. After the skirmish at Second River, the British occupied Hackensack and set about posting guards and pickets in the surrounding neighborhoods. One such was at New Bridge, apparently in Robert Timpany's schoolhouse. A small guard from the British Fifty-second and Fifty-seventh Regiments of Foot had drawn the notice of Lieutenant Colonel Aaron Burr, commanding a detachment of seventy-five men from Malcolm's Additional Continental Regiment at Ramapo. First Lieutenant Alexander Dow related their enterprise:

> *When the moon was down, and by full consent of Officers made [a] secret and sudden attack. Imagining them to be one hundred strong, Coll Burr proportioned our different attacks in platoons, he pitched mine to Enter first without any alarm and Challenge the whole to surrender which I did, that moment finding them both Brave and Obstinate, as they flew to their arms I dropped three of them with my Bayonet on the muzzle of my fusee by this time one stout fellow attacked me in the same manner But I parried him off and in his endeavoring to disarm me he Bit several holes in the Barrel of my fusee, whilst my worthy Serjeant Williams Came to my relief and stabbed him Dead, I then turned on another full armed who begged for mercy I bid him surrender his arms to me which he did into my hand, by this time the rest of our party had done their part and taken one more prisoner.*

The picket was also in the crosshairs of the local Continental militia, who, according to Militiaman David Ritzema Bogert, arrived on the scene afterward: "I was there then 18 of the company with Lieutenant [Adam] Boyd, were sent to surprize the British picquet…& when we came into the guard house (Tenpenny's School house) we found it empty. Colonel Burr had taken the picket without firing & carried them away and the Enemy seemed then not to know their picket was taken."

The enterprise was militarily insignificant, the British losing five men as prisoners with only a few others killed and wounded, but it raised Rebel morale for the time being.

The war continued on, with many raids on Staten Island through the end of the year, particularly on November 27, 1777, when three officers of the battalion were surprised and taken prisoner, including Abraham Van Buskirk's son, Lieutenant Jacob Van Buskirk. Months of skirmishes, disease, desertion, prisoners and discharges had taken their toll through the battalions. A smallpox epidemic from February to March 1778 swept through the Fourth Battalion, killing over forty men. On April 25, 1778, in response to the many losses and difficulty in recruiting, the six battalions of New Jersey Volunteers were reduced to four. For Van Buskirk's battalion, it meant their ten companies were reduced and consolidated to only five, with the supernumerary officers placed upon half-pay and retired until vacancies occurred, or they were provided for in some other way. Most interestingly, both majors, Robert Timpany and Daniel Isaac Browne, were put on half-pay, and a new major was brought in, Philip Van Cortland of Hanover, Morris County. Van Cortland had joined the regiment early on, serving as major-of-brigade to Brigadier General Skinner. Van Cortland would continue as major of the battalion for the remainder of the war.

For Major Timpany, life *en second* could not have been enjoyable given his former activity. After a year and a half in limbo at his new residence at 6 Maiden Lane in New York City (along with Captain Samuel Hayden and Surgeon Henry Dougan of the New Jersey Volunteers, also on the half-pay list), Timpany was ordered to join the British expedition to take Charleston, South Carolina. In a letter he wrote to Robert McCulloh of the Provincial Inspector General's Office, we gain some insight into his role and desires in this campaign:

James Island 5ᵗʰ March 1780

Dear Sir

I embrace this Opportunity Pr. Capt. Wells to acquaint you of my arrival at this place after a passage of nine weeks. I am at present nothing more than a Volunteer my Old friend the Col. recommended my Comeing and my anxious desire to be once more on Service prompd. me also. At Present the Situation is not the most agreeable having left my Baggage at North Edisto with the rest belonging to the Army. We are Fortifying & Building Batteries on this Side Ashly River in sight of the Rebell Fleet and Garrison, we proceed Slow but I hope Shure. My next I expect will be dated in Charlestown. The bearer of this will deliver you a letter for the Inspector Genl. It gave me pleasure to hear of your promotion and the respectable Character the Gentlemen from Savanah gave you at New York.

Write to me the First Opportunity. If Collonel [Alexander] Innis is not left Savanah you would Oblige me in mentioning my name. If he intends any thing for me I think he will acquaint you.
I am your Very Hbl. Servt.
R Timpany

His services did not go unrewarded. After the city was taken, marking Britain's greatest victory of the war, Sir Henry Clinton appointed Major Timpany to act as second in command to the famous Patrick Ferguson in organizing and regulating the South Carolina Militia. Ferguson likewise commanded a number of Timpany's friends from the New Jersey Volunteers, serving in a temporary corps of rangers styled the American Volunteers. Amongst this corps was Timpany's old Lieutenant Martin Ryerson, who died in Savannah on February 7, 1780, "after 32 Days Sickness of a Nervis Complaint…Accationed in a great Measure by Sea Sickness." While not specifically a part of the American Volunteers, Timpany signed a contingent account receipt for the forty-odd men of the Fourth Battalion attached to the corps, even though Captain Samuel Ryerson was officer officially in charge of them.

Timpany's whereabouts and duties with the militia are a mystery for the rest of 1780. Thousands of South Carolinians had renewed their allegiance to the British after the fall of Charleston, with many taking up arms against them again whenever any considerable force of Continental troops appeared in their neighborhoods. For his part, Ferguson, along with the American Volunteers and about one thousand North and

South Carolina Militia, fought in numerous skirmishes throughout the Carolina backcountry until arriving at Kings Mountain, North Carolina. There, on October 6, 1780, Ferguson wrote his last letter, and it was to Major Timpany, confessing that the country around him swarmed with "an inundation of Barbarians." Ferguson showed deep concern as to the outcome of the battle he knew would soon be upon him, but showing confidence in his men: "We are inferior in Number but as to Quality." The next morning Ferguson was killed and his entire command killed or captured in the famous battle at Kings Mountain. Captain Samuel Ryerson lost his ring finger in the beginning of the battle, although he later boasted that "it Didnt hinder Me from keping the Field."

The last active service in which the Bergen County major was engaged was at Georgetown, South Carolina, when an enemy intelligence report listed the strength of the post in January 1781 as "Majr. Tenpenny's detacht. 80 [Men]." Tenpenny seems to have been how Timpany was nicknamed by friend and foe alike, as Patrick Ferguson addressed him by the same name. Timpany, who had been sick at the time of Kings Mountain and was evidently wounded at some point in the groin and foot, perhaps no longer felt the South Carolina climate was healthy for him and requested leave to go to New York. His plans to recuperate his health were short-circuited by the French navy under Admiral DeGrasse, which captured his ship off the Capes of Virginia. The unfortunate major was paroled to New York City, where he, among others, was exchanged for Colonel deLaumoy, a French engineer in American service who had been captured in Charleston in 1780, where Timpany's southern adventure began.

The question remains why Major Timpany, a zealous and active officer, was removed from active command in 1778, replaced by a gentleman who was essentially a staff officer. One clue might be over-fondness of the bottle, as revealed in this anecdote provided after the war by John L. Mesereau in his application for a United States pension. Mesereau was engaged in spying for Congressional cause on Staten Island when he was discovered by some British soldiers:

> *The sentry hailed, and I fled on my hands and feet to a ditch, along which I could run without being much exposed to his fire. He fired his musket just as I got into the ditch, and his ball struck a post just over my head. I then jumped out of the ditch and ran directly to my lodgings. The Sentinel, with others, pursued me and reached the out door just as*

I entered my room. Had they persevered, I must have been discovered and taken. It happened, however that a British "Major Tenpenny" (so-called) quartered at the same house, and, being drunk at the time, countermanded further search, swearing "there were no rebels in the house where he lodged," or words to that effect.

However, drinking, even hard drinking, was usually tolerated in the army's officers and even considered a social norm.

Another clue, or perhaps just an illustration as to how fortune had turned against the former teacher, is revealed in a pair of letters Timpany wrote to Captain Gideon White, a fellow Provincial officer and merchant who sold goods to the army as well as extended cash to many of its officers. It would appear Major Timpany was among his clients:

New York 12th Decr. 1782
Dr. Sir
Be assured your Letter much distresses me, not on account of the Language, for it is certainly modest, but that it is not in my power to immediately answer the obligation I am under to you, when we meet next I hope I shall be able to give some satisfaction. Ever since I left Charlestown I have given half my Subsistance to satisfy some Gambling Debts, & that is not the worst, I am still under the same Embarrasment untill the 24th of this month come a Year—the other half I am obliged to subsist upon, & as I draw nothing but the bare pay You may think it is a close living—I will refer saying anything more till I see you.
& am with Sincerity Your much
Obliged Friend &c.
R. Timpany

Capt. [Gideon] White

The second letter showed the major's situation as not having improved in the slightest degree:

Sir,
I recd. Yours Yesterday morning should be glad I could answer it, but it being entirely out of my power must bear the consequence of your threats—I have recd. no money since I saw you, and had none then, And untill the Commander in Chief gives an Order for my Baggage lost I am

not able to pay, As one half of my Pay is already out of my hands,—I have not the least objections to Your making Application as I heartily wish You to be paid.
I am Your very Humble Servt.
Robt. Timpany
25th March 1783
Capt. [Gideon] *White*

The end of the war meant a new beginning for Robert Timpany. While no property confiscation was made against him in Bergen County, he had no home to return to in 1783. With the Provincial Corps' reduction, all its officers were promised half-pay for life, and all Loyalists could expect free grants of land from the British. For Major Timpany, this land would be in Digby, Nova Scotia. Timpany, along with his wife, Sarah, two children under ten years old and five servants, set sail from New York on board the transport ship *Atalanta*, forever leaving America.

After several years' residence at Digby, the Timpany family moved to the head of St. Mary's Bay and eventually on to Yarmouth. The ties to Bergen County were still present, however, as his daughter Charlotte married Gabriel Bidder Van Norden, son of Gabriel Van Norden, a noted Loyalist from Hackensack who had likewise sought a continuance of British government in Nova Scotia.

Timpany's wounds and ill state of health from the Revolution did little to affect his final days. Major Timpany was among the last of the officers of the Revolution still alive when he finally passed away in 1844, at the remarkable age of 102 years old, "retaining his faculties to the end of life, and reading without the use of spectacles."

———•———

Todd Braisted is a lifelong resident of Bergen County. He has served as president of the Bergen County Historical Society, chairman of the West Point Chapter of the Company of Military Historians and president of the 4th Battalion, New Jersey Volunteers reenactment group. In 2007 he was elected the first American to serve as honorary vice-president of the United Empire Loyalist Association of Canada. He has organized numerous living history commemorations in the county, including those at Historic New Bridge Landing and Fort Lee Historic Park. A contributing author of the 1999 Garland Book Moving On: Black Loyalists in the Afro-Atlantic World, *he has also been the author of numerous journal articles. He likewise lectures extensively on Loyalist and local history. He currently serves on the editorial board and as columnist for* American Revolution Magazine *and has also appeared as a guest historian on the popular PBS show* History Detectives *and the CBC's* Who Do You Think You Are? *His wife, Susan Braisted, is a longtime reenactor and co-founder of* In Good Company, *an eighteenth-century dance group.*

"IT APPEARED TO ME AS IF HERE WE SHOULD LIVE SECURE"

A Family's Precarious Refuge in Paramus, 1776 to 1780

JOHN U. REES

Accounts of military actions and soldiers' experiences during our founding conflict are numerous; less often do we hear from the civilians who stood in the way of war. Helen Kortright Brasher was the wife of Colonel Abraham Brasher, an officer in the New York militia, early war Congressman and member of the State Assembly from September 1777 until his death in 1783. Mrs. Brasher recorded her Revolutionary narrative in 1802 when she was sixty-three; her recollections are vivid, engaging and, where they can be verified, reliable.

The Brasher family, including Helen's mother, sixty-eight-year-old Hester Cannon Kortright, and children—Judith, age fifteen; Elizabeth, age nine; and one-year-old Gasherie—resided in New York City when the war began. The colonel first served in the Continental Congress for three years, starting in 1775. From the beginning he was involved in local politics, and Mrs. Brasher wrote of the time,

> At this time the unhappy dispute between Great Britain and the Colonys began. My husband being a warm American...openly espoused her cause...the storm thickened and all our domestick happiness appeared at an end. The zeal of my husband was so great, that his family which before had been his sole care and pleasure...now became only...secondary...He would often say, my country first and then my family. In this we differed. I thought a mans family should and ought to be his first object.

Eventually, admitting "my politicks were the same as his," she relented in her objections, telling her husband, "Go my dear, and serve your country I will find the means to provide for the family."

Following the British evacuation of Boston in March 1776, Continental forces moved south to New York. Helen Brasher noted,

> *Our peaceful city became a garrisoned town, General* [George] *Washington…arrived…and nothing was seen or heard but preparations for war, the pavements of our streets were taken up, fortifications erected, at last, by order of Genl. Washington all the women and children were ordered to leave it, my husband procured part of a house for us at Hackensack in Jersey, to it we retired with my aged mother three children and three servants* [including Thomas, a slave], *my husband still in the city and its environs. My anxiety on his account was great. The British got possession of the City, my husband got over to us, and I felt once more happy. My husband was chosen a member of the Assembly. They sat at Esopus* [modern-day Kingston, New York] *a great distance from us.*

With the tide turning against the Whig cause, and Crown forces crossing into New Jersey, the colonel's wife recalled,

> *Our situation became very public by the troops from Long Island and York Island all crossing over to the Jerseys. My husband proposed moving us farther back in the country, he got rooms for us at Paramus* [now Hohokus, Bergen County, New Jersey], *a village about twelve miles back. To this retired place he removed us at a Mr. John Hoppers, it appeared to me as if here we should live secure…from wars alarms.*

The Brasher family's move to Paramus soon placed them in the midst of occupying troops and military movements; lucky for them, they largely involved forces on the side of independence. December 1776 brought the first substantial military presence at Paramus, when troops under Major General William Heath took post there on the sixteenth. Jonathan Heart, doing duty as "Barack Master," recorded "The Troops under Command of Majr Genl Heath assigned to Quarters":

> *Maj Genl Heath to Garret Hoppers House—*
> *BD* [Brigadier] *Genl Parsons to a House near the Church—*
> *Colo Prescotts Regiment with Capt Lt. Treadwells Compy of the* [artillery] *Train in the Houses next adjacent to the Church—*
> *Colo Huntingtons & Tylers Regiments in the Houses next south of Genl Parsons Quarters—*

John U. Rees

Colo Ward.s Regt. in Houses on the Road North of the Church
Colo Wyllyss Regt with Capt Lt. Bryons Compy of the [artillery]
Train in the Houses next south of Head Quarters
The Light Horse in the House next North of Head Quarters

A December 21 return of Heath's two brigades, commanded by Generals

Samuel Parsons and George Clinton, shows a total strength of 2,479 troops; of that number only 966 were actually present at Paramus, the remainder being "on command" (on detached duty), sick, absent or on furlough. That same day General Heath informed General Washington he was moving his Continental regiments to Peekskill, New York, leaving General Clinton "with about 1000 of the Militia of Orange & Ulster Counties ordered out by the Convention of the State of New York...to guard for the present, this post, & the passes of the Highlands on this side of Hudson's River." After Clinton's forces left, the New Jersey militia kept a contingent at Paramus when Continental troops were not in garrison.

Historic marker on Glen Avenue, Ridgewood. *Courtesy of Ira Lieblich.*

The following year proved relatively uneventful, save for an unsuccessful May 1777 attempt to surprise a force of militia by the Loyalist New Jersey Volunteers, and British foraging operations in and around nearby Hackensack that September. Even the presence of substantial numbers of pro-British residents in the area did not prevent Mrs. Brasher, her children and retinue from making themselves relatively comfortable in their new residence.

> *Our landlord* [John Hopper] *was a miller, our bread and water was sure, and more than this we was not entitled to expect...* [When Colonel Brasher left for Esopus, New York] *I went to the apartment of my landlord and told him I put my mother selfe and children under his protection and flattered myselfe he would be a father and friend to us, he said he*

33

Damian Charpentier, natural resource interpretive technician, Fort Lee Historic Park. Soft or hard bread, usually baked in masonry ovens, was a staple foodstuff for eighteenth-century soldiers and civilians alike. *Courtesy of Ira Lieblich.*

would. I found him as good as his word…His wife [Mary] *was a fine humane woman whom I really loved…We passed our time as agreeable and happy as we could wish. We got acquainted with the neighbors, found them very good kind hospitable farmers. We had likewise in the vicinity of our habitation three or four families from New York who had daughters about the age of* [Judith] *my eldest, they became intimately acquainted… Her young companions often visited her and she them. My second daughter* [Elizabeth] *soon found playmates of her own and all promised fair to make our exile comfortable. My good mother soon got acquainted with the farmers wives as she spoke the Dutch language perfectly. She became a great favorite with all the neighboring men women and children. Everything that was offered for sale was first brought to our house so they could converse with her and she had the preference. We spent a very happy year in this village in peace and harmony.*

Perhaps not quite twelve months of peace. Writing of the year 1777, Mrs. Brasher told of several enemy incursions (probably including the New Jersey Volunteers raid), which likely led to the eventual decision for a Continental army post at Paramus and Hopperstown. Of that autumn she noted,

Our situation became very alarming, we had two or three of those nocturnal visits from the British. I wrote to my husband requesting him to come and remove us, as I found myself in a situation not to bear those frequent alarms at a time I should require entire composure and his company. He requested me to come to Esopus [where he served in the New York Assembly] *as it was impossible for him to leave it.*

Leaving her mother and the rest of her family at the Hopper home, Helen Brasher traveled with her eldest daughter to join her husband at Esopus. Soon after their arrival they witnessed the burning of the town by Crown forces on October 16, 1777. Following that harrowing experience, they returned to New Jersey in company with the colonel and "concluded to remain at Paramus till we could procure more secure accommodations."

In early summer 1778 the Brasher family's comparative peace was again disturbed by elements of Washington's army as it moved north after the Battle of Monmouth, and again that autumn when Continental forces under Major General William Alexander, Lord Stirling, gathered at Paramus to counter another enemy expedition to gather forage and food in Bergen County. In December 1778, Colonel Thomas Clark's 650-man North Carolina

Brigade was ordered to Paramus. Their occupation was the beginning of a rotating garrison of Continental troops that would last until spring of 1780. (Among the forces at Paramus during the summer, autumn and winter of 1779 were Major Henry Lee's Legion, Colonel William Washington's Third Continental Light Dragoons, elements of Lord Stirling's Division, the Light Infantry (comprising some 700 men) under Brigadier General Anthony Wayne and, that December, a mixed detachment under Lieutenant Colonel William DeHart, Second New Jersey Regiment.) Mrs. Brasher noted the hustle and bustle of military traffic:

> *At last* [Paramus] *became the route of our army. This totally changed the scene, from the simple whistle of the village lad and the cheerful song of the simple pleasant country girls, we had the fife the drum and all the accompaniments of noisy Mars. Our army frequently passed and repassed, at last it became the outpost of our army, a detachment always quartered there, our house constantly filled with officers amongst them many of our citizens. We could not refuse them quarters and it was my wish to make them as comfortable as I could. One party no sooner gone than another came. At last it became a perfect encampment, we had not a moment we could call our own, nor did I complain, so great was my zeal to promote all in my power the comfort or pleasure of my countrymen that were exposing their lives for their countrys safety.*

After giving birth to twins Abraham and Helen on December 19, 1779 (increasing their surviving offspring to five), Mrs. Brasher recalled,

> *My husband and faithful nurse left me, the Spring advanced and with it all our military noise and parade, and with them all our fears of the British. Our situation became truly alarming, continual skirmishes with the British and our troops nigh us…I wrote to my husband to come and remove us…He came and we were to look out for more secure quarters. He wrote to his friends at Morristown to procure a place for us. They said in a few weeks there would be apartments ready. This unfortunately detained us. I felt very uneasy about my husbands being at this time at home fearing if the enemy should come they would undoubtedly take him prisoner, and perhaps murder him. I frequently begged him not to sleep at home as they always surprised us at the dead of the night.*

While her recollections were written some twenty years after the event, Helen Brasher claims to have had forebodings regarding the danger at Paramus cum Hopperstown that winter. In any case, an unsuccessful March 23, 1780 British attack on the post would have done nothing to ease any fears she had. Here she recounts her misgivings in more detail:

> *At this period* [April 1780] *we had in the house a Maj. Boiles* [Thomas Lambert Byles, Third Pennsylvania Regiment], *who commanded a detachment that quartered in the neighborhood, and his guard lay in our kitchen. This my good husband thought a security to us but to me it appeared a sure omen of distress and frequently declared my fears to him and the Maj. by saying that I was sure his being in the house with his men would bring destruction on me and my family. The Maj. promised to remove himself and his men the next day, and said, Madam I will ensure your safety this night. I could not prevail upon my husband to leave the house that night as the Maj. had assured us of safety, but my fears was not to be so easyly lulled. My husband went to bed and I went to secure all the valuable articles in the house, my husband and my mother frequently calling to me and requesting me to go to bed, but I could not. I had got my trunks that had been removed back, in expectation of leaving this place, those greatly perplexed me knowing if they were taken from us we could not replace them. I went into the apartment of my landlord and begged him to get up and take his waggon and horses and my trunks and remove them a few miles up the country with some of his family apparel, that I felt confident that the enemy would be up that night and we would be plundered of all our clothing and it would be the means of securing his horses and himself. He laughed at my fears, said, in the morning he would, but this night there was no fear. Not being able to get assistance I went to bed but could not sleep from apprehension.*

The detailed description of the ensuing attack by a noncombatant is quite remarkable when laid alongside narratives of soldiers at the scene. Added to that, given the treatment she and her family endured, Mrs. Brasher's recounting is surprisingly restrained and evenhanded.

> *About two in the morning* [of April 16, 1780] *I was alarmed by the sound of many horses over a small bridge within ten or twelve yards of our house. I awoke my husband, saying arise my dear, I hear the British horse crossing the bridge, he arose, but before he could get on his clothing*

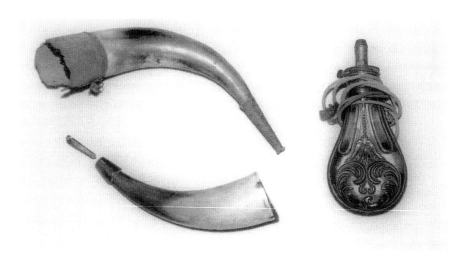

Powder horns were sometimes carried on campaign by Revolutionary militia or riflemen, but were more often used to store excess gunpowder. *Courtesy of the Schoolhouse Museum, Ridgewood, New Jersey. Ira Lieblich, photographer.*

we heard a tremendous firing of small arms, and a call to surrender or we will put you all to the bayonet. My husband left my room with his apparel in his hands and I knew not where he had gone. Our Maj. not knowing the number of the British ordered his men to fire out of the garret windows. Immediately the house was surrounded and the [musket] balls flew in every direction. I could not leave my room it being on the ground floor nor could I get to my aged mother and children who slept in a room opposite to mine separated by a small entry with a back door. I was so palsied by fright and consternation that I knew not what to do, at last the firing ceased and I ventured out to seek my husband mother and children. As I opened the door the first thing that presented itself to my sight was Maj. Boiles laying on the floor weltering in his blood. Humanity led me to him,—the house was full of men plundering everything they saw. I went to raise the Maj. but had not strength. Oh madam, he said, they have cruelly wounded me after I surrendered, and I have surely brought destruction on you and your amiable family. If I survive I will endeavor to compensate you. Pray Maj. do not mention this. Pray soldiers assist me to lift this gentleman on his bed,—they refused. An officer stepped up and assisted me to get him on the bed. They were writing his parole as he was too badly wounded to take with them. I was so totally occupied as almost to forget myself and family. At last [I] asked Maj. Boiles what had become of my husband. He replied he had not seen him that morning.

Good God! what had become of him, I went up to the commanding officer of the party and on my knees entreated him to let me know where my husband was, whether he was taken or whether slain. He sternly drove me from him saying he knew him not. I flew to the apartment of my mother and children found their room so crowded with soldiers plundering drawers trunks etc. that it was impossible to get to the bed of my mother who lay quiet as a lamb. My two girls were contending with the soldiers to save a few things, my son [Gasherie] *sat up in bed his little countenance distorted with surprise and resentment. I saw nothing of my husband. Almost distracted, I screamed out to my eldest daughter, my dear Judy what is become of your father. She silently gave me a signal for caution, and silence on that subject. I guessed he must be concealed in that room, I went back to the Maj.s apartment and to my utter horror and astonishment found the apartment all in flames, he still laying in his bed* [the wooden roof of the stone house having been set alight by the attackers to force Major Byles to surrender]. *I enquired of the British officer whether I had not permission to leave the house with my children and infirm mother, he said no, there were some of the dm^d rebels concealed in the house,* [and] *if they did not make their appearance we should all be consumed in the flames. I asked is this wounded officer to be likewise left to be consumed, they said they intended taking him to the next house. I endeavored once more to get into the apartment of my mother and children to do* [so] *I had to encounter the flames, had my handkerchief burned on my neck, my clothes scorched and my hands burned in several places. When I reached my mothers apartment I found it likewise in flames the curtains around her bed on fire and the room in so thick a smoke I could hardly perceive my children—found my husband up and dressed /* the [Crown forces] *had left the inside of the house* [and] *had drawn* [up in] *a rank in front and rear with their bayonets fixed to prevent anyone going out. My husband desired me to call the commanding officer and he would surrender. I begged him not, he said we must or we should all be consumed. My eldest daughter was so faint with the smoke as almost to be suffocated. I led her to the back door for air. One of the subaltern officers came up to me and offered his canteen with water / saying this is too much to see beauty in distress* [he] *ordered his men to draw back and let the lady and her daughter out, he took her by the hand and supported her. I slipped back to beg my husband be of good cheer they are going to leave us* [out] *I thought. I got my mother up and begged the wench to assist me in getting her bed out to secure it from the*

Soldiers used canteens to carry water and other beverages. This example is wooden; British canteens were usually made of tin. *Courtesy of the Schoolhouse Museum, Ridgewood, New Jersey. Ira Lieblich, photographer.*

flames. As the wench had hold of it by the two corners and I by the other two my husband proposed crouching under it. I was apprehensive, but he persisted and we dragged it out he remaining on hands and knees creeping under; we got it and him safe a few yards from the house; the wench returned with my mother. I ran for the children and by this strategem my husband got safe out unperceived in the presence of two hundred British troops with their bayonets fixed. We had scarcely left the house before the roof fell in and all was in a light flame. The British gave three cheers and left us. All lay on my poor husband, [who] we soon released and congratulated him on his miraculous escape.

The colonel and his family were left with their lives and little else, and grateful enough for that. His wife related the denouement:

We found our good landlord a little way from his house laying for dead with many bayonet wounds, but he recovered [John Hopper's wife Mary said nothing of his wounding, only that he "escaped at the time with the loss of his hat"], *not so poor Maj. Boiles, his wounds proved fatal, he died the next day. Our little army rallied and with the militia pursued the British killed and wounded many, retook many of our men and two waggons of plunder. Now was my distressed family left as it appeared, with nothing but the earth for their bed and the canopy of heaven for their*

40

covering, the hospitable mansion that sheltered them from many storms reduced to ashes, its worthy owner laying not far from it to all appearance dead. Great God, what a sight!…There was my husband, my children, my mother and my domesticks all alive around me petrifyed with fright and astonishment. This was surely a matter of joy and gratitude…the neighbors flocked around us all kindly offering to take us to their homes, we accepted the offer of our nighest as my mother could not walk far. We had not been above three or four houres at our neighbors, when our worthy friend, Mr. Fell who lived two miles from us came with his wagon and took us all to his house. There we remained till our friends at a distance heard of our situation.

Following their stay at Mr. Fell's house (either Judge John Fell or Colonel Peter Fell), the family was split. Helen Brasher's mother, daughter Elizabeth and eldest son Gasherie lived for a short while with Mr. Garret Abeel of Little Falls, New Jersey (on the Passaic River, three miles south of the Great Falls at modern-day Paterson). They were then sheltered for several years by Mrs. Brasher's brother-in-law Richard Willing at his home near Philadelphia, Pennsylvania. Mrs. Brasher, her husband, eldest daughter Judith and the twins moved to Morristown, New Jersey, into "the upper part of a large house of Mr. Jacob Arnold"; this was Arnold's Tavern, on the Morristown Green, where General Washington had stayed during the winter of 1777. Abraham Brasher died in Morristown in 1782. Afterward Helen sent for her mother and

we removed from Morristown to Newark to be nearer New York. My mother arrived, and in her good company I found great relief. The November following we removed to New York, but Oh!…changed did everything appear…We got possession of our houses, but they were racked, abused and filthy. My widowed situation made everything appear gloomy…Every returning exile appeared rejoiced. I could not join them, my happiness was at an end. The Lord in mercy to my children, enabled me to struggle through.

In order to support her family after returning to the city, Mrs. Brasher operated a dry goods store on 88 William Street, "near Maiden Lane," continuing in that business into the early 1790s. She outlived both sons and her eldest daughter but saw her middle and youngest daughters marry and prosper. Helen Kortright Brasher died in the city of New York in November 1819, seventeen years after writing her memoir of the war.

John Rees's version of Mrs. Brasher's story is dedicated to his mother, Virginia L. "Dolly" Rees. Her love of reading and abiding interest in the lives of both loved ones and strangers surely influenced his desire to tell stories of ordinary soldiers and civilians in wartime, and fueled his fascination for "small things forgotten."

Mr. Rees gives special thanks to Todd W. Braisted, a fine gentleman and good friend.

John Rees's work, focusing primarily on the common soldiers' experience during the War for Independence and North American soldiers' food from 1755 to the present, has appeared in the **ALHFAM** Bulletin *(Association of Living History, Farm, and Agricultural Museums),* The Brigade Dispatch *(journal of the Brigade of the American Revolution),* The Continental Soldier *(journal of the Continental Line),* Gastronomica: The Journal of Food and Culture, Journal of the Johannes Schwalm Historical Association, Military Collector & Historian, Minerva: Quarterly Report on Women and the Military, Muzzleloader Magazine, On Point: The Newsletter of the Army Historical Foundation *and* Percussive Notes *(journal of the Percussive Arts Society). He is a regular columnist for the quarterly newsletter* Food History News; *wrote four entries for the* Oxford Encyclopedia of American Food and Drink *and thirteen entries for the revised Thomson Gale edition of* Boatner's Encyclopedia of the American Revolution; *and contributed a chapter to Carol Karels's* The Revolutionary War in Bergen County *(2007). A partial article list plus many complete works are available online at www.revwar75. com/library/rees. Mr. Rees was elected Fellow of the Company of Military Historians in April 2009.*

Helen Kortright Brasher's complete recounting may be read in "The Narrative of Mrs. Abraham Brasher (Helen Kortright), Giving an Account of her Experiences During the Revolutionary War" (1802), typed manuscript in the collections of the New York Historical Society, 170 Central Park West, New York, NY, 10024 (www.nyhistory.org/ web/).

Mr. Rees's monograph on the April 16, 1780 Hopperstown attack may be read in a later chapter in this book.

Campbell's Tavern

A Hackensack Landmark in Revolutionary War Days

Kevin Wright

On Saturday morning, September 13, 1873, wreckers commenced an arduous assault upon the old "stone fortress in the heart of the village." But Campbell's Tavern, long a Hackensack landmark, would not go easily and would not die alone.

Many inhabitants dawdled about the dusty scene, each one having "a story to relate of what he knows about its history." Schoolboys probed the crumpled hulk, believing that hidden treasures lay somewhere buried in its foundation. Onlookers encouraged the young prospectors in hopes "that something would be found to indicate the date of erection of the building"—but the mystery endured as no interesting clues or relics were unearthed.

For most townsfolk, the quaint old Dutch tavern evoked a flood of memories. It was fondly recognized as the "theatre of many events, which have been lost to history" in a *Bergen County Democrat* article six days later. But its origins remained the object of much conjecture as no old-timer could guess how long it had stood at the corner of Main and Morris Streets.

At the time of its demise, the only light that octogenarian Samuel Dawson could shed on the subject was to say "that when he was young it was an old house." Its exterior had been updated to suit changing architectural tastes, but demolition bared the antique methods and materials of its anatomy—thick stone walls and heavy hand-hewn timbers—and further fed public surmise as to its age. Henry D. Winton, publisher of the *Bergen County Democrat,* offered his observations of the building's construction, noting, "Lime was of little use in the mixture of mortar in those days, and there is barely a sprinkling of it in the laying up of the foundations. The timbers were as sound as when the house was put up, consisting of oak and white wood. The [plaster] walls and ceilings were six inches in thickness, and made of a mixture of clay and straw, which answered the same purpose as hair and lime does in mortar at the present time. The lath were split out of oak, and looked more like wagon staves than ceiling lath."

On April 13, 1751, merchant Abraham Ackerman purchased a lot on the west side of the King's Road, now Main Street, Hackensack, measuring 62 feet wide and 100 feet deep, from blacksmith and County Judge Jacob Titsort for four pounds. The property was bounded north by land of Barent De Boogh, west by the remaining land of Jacob Titsort and south "by the Lane [now Morris Street] that now leads to [Jacob Titsort's] house." Ackerman's brownstone house, built on a corner of the Hackensack Green in 1751, stood nearly opposite and only 150 feet distant from the Bergen County Court House erected in 1731.

The documentary record is silent for two decades after Ackerman's construction of the stone dwelling. Then, on January 11, 1771, Archibald Campbell mortgaged "All that Messuage, Tenement and Land…on the West Side of the King's Road near the Court House" to John Vanderbilt of New York for £200 in New York currency. According to the mortgage deed, the boundary survey of the tavern lot began at the King's Road—now Main Street, Hackensack—at the lane leading to the house lot of Barent De Boogh, running west 150 feet along this lane, then running south 62 feet along James Van Beuren's land to the lane that is now Morris Street, thence east 100 feet along this lane to the King's Road and finally turning north along the road 62 feet to the beginning point.

Archibald Campbell was born on the Isle of Man and settled at Hackensack in 1765 at the conclusion of the French and Indian War. His wife, Catherine, born in Northern Ireland, arrived in 1768 with their eldest son, Robert, then only four years old. Three more children were born to the couple, namely, John (1770), George (1772) and Hannah.

REVOLUTIONARY WAR ASSOCIATIONS

Though the tavern's age was a matter of speculation, its associations with the Revolutionary War were common knowledge and a prized piece of village folklore. The oldest inhabitants would confidently relate how "during the revolutionary war it was occupied as a public house, and a sort of refuge for the Tories." Its proprietor, Archibald Campbell, "had the honor of furnishing supplies for the table of General Washington who was then occupying the residence of Peter Zabriskie, opposite (now the Mansion House property) as his headquarters." Some recollections were particularly vivid, spilling from memory onto the pages of history. Robert Campbell, Archibald's thirteen-year-old son, painted with words a scene about Campbell's Tavern in the autumnal gloaming of those trying times:

> *After the evacuation of Fort Lee, in November, 1776, and the surrender of Fort Washington, Washington, at the head of his army (about 3,000), entered Hackensack about dusk. The night was dark, cold and rainy; but I had a fair view of them from the light of the windows as they passed on our side of the street. They marched two abreast; looked ragged—some without shoes to their feet, and most wrapped in blankets. Washington then and for some time previous had his headquarters at the residence of Peter Zabriskie, a private house, the supplies for the General's table being furnished by Archibald Campbell, the tavernkeeper.*
>
> *The next evening, after the Americans had passed through, the British were encamped on the opposite side of the river. We could see their fires about 100 yards apart, gleaming brilliantly at night, extending some distance below the town and more than a mile up toward New Bridge. Washington was still at his quarters, and had with him his suite, Life Guards, a company of foot, a regiment of cavalry and some soldiers from the rear of his army. In the morning, before he left, he rode down to the dock [of John Varick] where the bridge now is, viewed the enemy's encampment some 10 or 15 minutes, and then returned to Mr. Campbell's door and called for some wine and water. After he had drunk, and when Mr. Campbell was taking the glass from him, the latter, with tears streaming down his face, said: "Gen., what shall I do? I have a family of small children and a little property here; shall I leave it?" Washington kindly took his hand and replied: "Mr. Campbell, stay by your property and keep neutral." Then bidding him good-bye, rode off. About noon next day the British took possession of the town, and in the afternoon the Green was covered with Hessians—a horrid, frightful sight to the inhabitants. There were between 3,000 and 4,000, with their whiskers, brass caps, and kettles or brass drums. A part of these same troops were two months later taken prisoners at Trenton.*

If indeed Washington did counsel neutrality, he did so loudly enough to lull the suspicion of unfriendly eavesdroppers, for sullen Tories were reportedly numerous in the little county town. Mr. Campbell's taproom might prove a well of useful intelligence in the days and weeks ahead. Protestations

Revolutionary War–era tavern in Jersey City (then part of Bergen County). *Courtesy of Kevin Wright.*

of neutrality, however, did not dissuade the Crown forces, which poured into town in the Americans' wake, for they emptied his larder, linen closet, fowl pens and barn. The British and their Loyalist allies made off with Archibald's horses, potatoes, turnips, turkeys, ducks, fowls, sheets, pillow cases, tablecloths, towels, shirts and shifts, handkerchiefs, cravats, gown and trousers. They burned twenty-six panels of new five-rail fence in their campfires and vandalized his back house.

But even the bleak field of war offered opportunities to the watchful eye. On May 16, 1778, Archibald Campbell paid one hundred pounds to Hendrick Bosch for ten acres of land along the public road leading from town down to the Hackensack Ferry. As he was soon reminded, cash and valuables could easily be carried away and only the land safely remained. According to claims submitted for his losses during the war, Archibald Campbell had a japanned server taken in 1777, and he paid a guinea to retrieve a stolen mare. In October 1778, the enemy absconded with the Campbells' milk cow, sheep, shoats, pigs, fowls, smoked pork, fresh pork, potatoes, sheets, shirts, stocks, shifts, aprons, summer clothes, trousers, stockings, a petticoat, a half gallon of rum and twenty gallons of cider.

But the worst was yet to come. The winter of 1779–80 exceeded any in memory for severity, and the Continental army, encamped at Morristown, suffered from the deprivations of proper clothing and provisions. To protect his line of communications with West Point and New England and to gather intelligence on enemy movements around Manhattan, Washington posted a small body of troops at Paramus.

Throughout the long, deep winter, Tories in the neighborhood and disillusioned deserters relayed detailed intelligence on the disposition and strength of the American outpost to New York City. The British command contemplated a surprise attack but was inhibited by harsh weather. A January blizzard buried the countryside. Using sleighs, American and British troops skirmished across the frozen bay between Elizabethtown and Staten Island.

The waterways remained frozen until late February. Spring was slow in coming and a heavy mantle of snow still covered the ground in March. On March 18, 1780, Major Christopher Stuart of the Fifth Pennsylvania Regiment, commanding a regiment made up of detachments from several regiments, relieved the guard at Paramus and purposely took up quarters in the homes of British sympathizers living near Paramus Church. To provide an alarm in case of an enemy advance, Captain John Outwater's militia company was ordered to Hackensack.

As the weather improved, a pincer attack was launched from Manhattan against the Continental regiment at Paramus. It was not unanticipated. As the *New-York Gazette and the Weekly Mercury* publicly stated on March 27, 1780, four days after the raid, the target was "sundry new fangled Justices of the Peace, who had assembled there [at Hackensack] to devise means to harass and distress such of their neighbors as were thought to be disaffected to the cause of rebellion." On March 22, 1780, four judges joined Sheriff Adam Boyd, Adjutant Cornelius Haring and four militia officers in seeking protection from Major Stuart and the Continental troops posted at Paramus because the militia was stretched too thin for adequate warning and defensive countermeasures. They intimated "that the Enemy have in Contemplation to make an Attack & Incursion on the Inhabitants of Hackensack within a few Days" and presciently suggested "that the Security of your Detachment in some measure depends on regular Scouts & Guards being kept up, near the Lines." They asked whether General Washington's orders would allow the American army to move closer for their protection, referring Major Stuart "to Lieutenant Colonel Varick, who is so good as to take charge of this in our behalf."

Three hundred men commanded by Lieutenant Colonel John Howard, of the First Regiment of Foot Guards, boarded boats at Spuyten Duyvil and landed at Closter. This column marched a roundabout route to Paramus

Church and Hoppertown by way of Werimus, intending to fall undetected upon the rear of the American cantonments there. Unfortunately, their transports were delayed three and a half hours by obstructions at Kingsbridge. Another three hundred British and Hessian troops, commanded by Lieutenant Colonel Duncan McPherson of the Royal Highland Regiment, landed at Weehawken. Captain Cornelius Hatfield, serving with the Royal Volunteer Militia, acted as a guide. Making their way undetected to Little Ferry, they passed the Hackensack River about midnight in a whaleboat and canoe to surprise the militia and sleeping magistrates in the town of Hackensack. Two dozen men from the Forty-third Regiment hurried through Hackensack to seize the new bridge and protect their avenue of retreat. About 3:00 a.m., the main body of the British column marched through the village, turning down the lane that is now the Passaic Street to Zabriskie's Mills in the Arcola section of Paramus at 5:30 a.m. to join the attack upon the American outpost at Paramus. Captain Thorn and a hundred soldiers, including about fifty Germans from the First Anspach-Bayreuth Regiment, remained behind with orders "to attack every house that should be pointed out to them by the guides and refugees."

The opportunity to settle old scores was at hand. Captain John Outwater's militia company, quartered for the night in the barracks, barns and outhouses of the village, was rudely awakened. Most hastened to safety across moonlit fields, but some had the presence of mind to mount their horses and ride off to alert the Continental outpost at Paramus.

The invaders set fire to Hackensack Court House and burned the dwellings of shoemaker John Chapple and Sheriff Adam Boyd. According to his claim for damages, John Chapple had "a House burnt down to the Ground, which contained two Rooms and an entry and a Milk House on the lower floor and on the Upper Story was Convenience for two Rooms more, the one being finished and the other not and a Good convenient Garret." It was appraised at £200. The County Court House, built in 1731, was forty-eight feet long and thirty feet wide. It was outfitted with a bell, installed in 1736, and a "clock and Hour Work," which was set in its steeple in 1763. As to the loss of the building and its furnishings, the county later claimed: "to Burning the Court House £500. To the town Clock £57.12s.0"

The attackers kicked in William Provoost's doors and took him prisoner. Reverend Dirck Romeyn, residing at the house of John Varick, escaped capture "by secreting behind the Chimney on the Collar beams." His brother John was made a prisoner. The wanton looting continued as soldiers "almost tore the house of Mr. Campbell, innkeeper, to pieces, after plundering him of a very considerable sum of specie and continental money. Their cruelty and brutality to the women was unparalleled; some they most inhumanly choked to make them tell where their money was; and one, we hear, was so unfortunate as to have her arm broke by them."

The stricken courthouse, standing on the west side of the Green, only 150 feet from Campbell's Tavern, spewed tongues of flame and gasps of glowing embers. Fortunately, the wind was from the west and Archibald's wife and children saved their home and livelihood by throwing water on the roof.

Archibald Campbell vividly recalled the events of that night. On November 2, 1782, he inventoried the losses he suffered at "about 4 o'clock in the morning" of March 23, 1780: 222 Spanish milled dollars; four thousand Continental dollars; silver tablespoons; silver teaspoons; a large silver punch ladle; large silver tea tongs; a silver watch, Dublin made, worth seven guineas; a silver sauce boat; another silver watch; a bag of old silver; a bag of copper; a satin cloak; a white cloak; a black silk hat; a white silk hat; a lawn apron; a gauze apron; handkerchiefs; a dress cap; a spring muslin cap; a pair of black silk gloves; burned china cups and saucers; a large china teapot; a burned china gallon bowl; half-gallon china bowl; china plates; women's stays; a mahogany tea chest full of Hyson tea; a child's dressing cape; and one fowling piece.

Due to "unavoidable delays," British Lieutenant Colonel McPherson and his troops appeared upon the road near Paramus Church at 7:15 a.m., too late to join in the action there. They arrived in time to see Colonel Howard's men pursuing the retreating Americans, but he was on the opposite bank of the Saddle River and unable to intercept the fugitives.

The British force returned to Zabriskie's Mills, where Captain Thorn and his prisoners were waiting. Prisoners included John Van Antwerp, John Bogart, William Provoost, Henry Van Winkle, G. Van Wagenen, Morris Earl, John Duryee, John Banta, Jacobus Brower, William Brower, John Van Giesen, Isaac VanValen, Peter Zabriskie, John Demarest, John Romeyn, Guilliam Barthoff, Jonathan Doremus and Christian Demarest. The slow train of men and wagons retraced their steps toward Hackensack, turned northeast on Main Street and slogged toward New Bridge. The parade comprised a stream of soldiers laden with sacks of plunder, wagons carrying the wounded and an unwilling gaggle of male prisoners under armed guard.

Major Christopher Stuart assembled about one hundred men at Paramus and began a cautious pursuit. About thirty infuriated militiamen joined, behaving "with great Spirit," according to Stuart's acknowledgement. The growing swarm of pursuers supposedly compelled the British "to run without Intermission from a Mile below the [Paramus] Church to the New Bridge (the Distance not less than Eleven Miles)." Peter Fell was instrumental in providing Stuart with "Knowledge of the Country," while coordinating the actions of the militia. Perhaps it was Fell who informed Stuart that "Friendly Inhabitants" would assemble at New Bridge and trap or delay the enemy "by hoisting or cutting away the Bridge."

The invaders tramped the soft road along the foot of the Red Hills to New Bridge. Flankers held the gathering swarm of Continental troops and militiamen at bay, who nonetheless took potshots at every opportunity. The small irregular force of Americans "pushed them, on their retreat, very hard, took a few prisoners, and killed and wounded several, whom they carried off in wagons." One American eyewitness reported, "the Enemy had three or four wagons full of killed and wounded—their retreat was so precipitate, that when any of their dead and wounded fell off the wagons, they did not tarry to take them up." In the running battle, several prisoners escaped. One Hessian musketeer on the retreat later wrote,

> We took considerable booty, both in money, silver watches, silver dishes and spoons and in household stuff, good clothes, fine English linen, silk stockings, gloves, handkerchiefs, with other precious [linen] goods, satin and stuffs. My own booty which I brought safely back, consisted of two silver watches, three sets of silver buckles, a pair of woman's cotton stockings, a pair of man's mixed Summer stockings, two shirts and four chemises of good English linen, two fine tablecloths, one silver tablespoon, and one teaspoon, [several] Spanish dollars, and six York shillings in money. The other part, viz., eleven [pillow cases] of fine linen, and more than two dozen handkerchiefs, with six silver plates and a silver drinking mug, which were tied together in a bundle, I had to throw away on account of our harried march, and [I left] them to the enemy that was pursuing us.

According to one account, the enemy, retiring from Red Mills and Hackensack, found the planks torn up from New Bridge and was delayed "two hours replacing them, during which time skirmishing was going on with those in pursuit." When they finally were able to pass the bridge, a rear guard again tore up the planks and posted themselves on an eminence on the other side to delay further pursuit by their tormentors. The columns split, marching either to Moore's Landing near Fort Lee or to Weehawken, at which places they embarked for Manhattan.

According to the "Return of the Killed, Wounded & Missing at the attack of the Rebel Troops at Paramus in Jersey, the 23rd March 1780," discovered by historian Todd Braisted in the Sir Henry Clinton Papers at the University of Michigan's William L. Clements Library, Captain David Anstruther of the Forty-second Regiment was wounded in action at New Bridge. In all, the invaders counted one killed, thirteen missing and eighteen wounded, including two wounded and ten missing Germans. Again, according to Braisted's research, Major Christopher Stuart reported three wounded and thirty-five missing, presumed captured ("Return of the wounded & missing of Continental Troops, 23 March 1780," Library of Congress, *George Washington Papers, Series 4, General Correspondence, 6 March 1780–24 April 1780*). The raiders brought sixty-two prisoners back to New York City, including twenty-four captured Continental soldiers and twenty-three militiamen.

The Bergen militia also suffered casualties. A musket ball struck Captain Outwater below the knee, a souvenir of battle that he carried to his grave. Hendrick Van Giesen, of Hackensack, was "wounded by a spent ball, which cut his upper lip, knocked out four front teeth, and was caught in his mouth."

Archibald Campbell's night was not over yet. His harrowing adventure was recounted in 1844: "This gentleman, who had been several weeks confined to his bed by rheumatism, they forced into the streets and compelled to follow them. Often in the rear, they threatened to shoot him if he did not quicken his pace. In the subsequent confusion he escaped and hid in the cellar of a house opposite New Bridge [that is, the Zabriskie-Steuben House]. He lived until 1798, and never experienced a return of the rheumatism."

In another version of these events, detailed in Reverend Theodore Romeyn's *Historical Discourse Delivered on Occasion of the Re-Opening and Dedication of the First Reformed (Dutch) Church at Hackensack, N.J. May 2, 1869,* Campbell escaped his captors standing in two feet of water beneath the new bridge, "which hydropathic treatment may account for the fact that he was cured of his painful disease, unless we may suppose that vigorous bodily exercise for two miles at the point of a bayonet, or a good thorough fright could serve as well as a curative."

The *New-York Gazette and the Weekly Mercury* put another spin on the night's events, reporting on April 3, 1780, "In the course of the march a Clergyman with another inoffensive inhabitant (taken prisoners by mistake) were dismissed and reported to have been accidentally shot by the Rebels." According to a report in the *New-York Packet and the American Advertiser* of Fishkill, New York, on March 30, 1780, Mr. Periam, tutor of the academy at Paramus, was badly wounded in the shoulder by American fire while a British prisoner.

AFTERLIFE

At war's end, the Bergen County Board of Justices and Freeholders met at the house of Archibald Campbell eight times between September 1783 and December 1787. In 1784 a new two-story County Court House, thirty feet wide and sixty feet long, was built on a lot donated by Peter Zabriskie on the east side of Main Street, bounded south by "a Certain Road [Bridge Street] intended to be laid out by the sd. Peter Zabriskie towards the Hackinsack River."

According to a report in the *New-Jersey Citizen*, Campbell's Tavern was long known as the "Albany Stage House," having been a stage depot for carrying passengers and mails between Manhattan and Albany. In the early days of the Republic, it became "Federal Headquarters" and was widely patronized by the legal fraternity in court times.

On August 28, 1797, Archibald Campbell was named Hackensack's first postmaster. His son George succeeded him as tavern keeper after his death on December 28, 1798. Tax ratables for New Barbados Township in 1802 list George, Catherine and Robert Campbell as inhabitants. George Campbell was appointed postmaster in 1803. Thereafter, the old stand was successively occupied by Brom Allen, John Baird, Brom Allen again, Widow (Catherine) Campbell, William Jones, Jacob J. Banta, Garry Bamper, James Vanderpool, William Van Beuren, Samuel Dawson, Victor W. Ramee and D.L. Edmonton. The tavern house of the widow Campbell is mentioned in a legal notice in the *Bee and Paterson Advertiser* on April 8, 1816. Documentary evidence also shows that William Jones was tavernkeeper from at least 1819 through 1822. In 1820 the tax ratables list Lawrence Van Orden, owner of a "stage," immediately after the name of William Jones.

The weathered old building was rejuvenated in April 1860 and divided into stores. Describing "Village Improvements," a reporter for the *Bergen County Journal* strolled Main Street and made note of the changes:

> *We come next to the old Campbell house, which in the hands of its present proprietor, Mr. John Feldman, seems to have renewed its youth. It would be difficult to recognize in the present modern-looking building, the old, quaint, Dutch tavern, before which, in "the times that tried men's souls," General Washington was wont to rein up his horse in order to taste old Archibald's applejack. As we have said, the building has been modernized: the high stoop is among the things that were; the short, unsightly windows, with solid board shutters, have expanded into large show windows which admit*

light to conveniently arranged stores; and the painters have also assisted in putting a very different complexion upon the edifice. One of the stores is occupied by Mr. Feldman as a cigar store and has been very nicely fitted up for that business. One of the others has been hired by Mr. S. Feder for a clothing store; and two stores, one 12 by 21 feet in size, and one 18 by 36 feet, (at the corner of Morris Street), are yet to be let.

On January 23, 1872, Samuel H. Campbell and Eliza Jane, his wife, of New Barbados Township, released the lot, "known as the old Tavern Stand," bounded by Main and Morris Streets, to John Feldman of Hoboken for $3,000, according to the *Bergen County Deed Book J8, 266.* In September 1873, Campbell's Tavern was razed to make way for the Bergen County Bank, a three-story brick building measuring twenty-five by seventy-five feet, which occupies the site to this day.

———•———

A native of Newton, New Jersey, Kevin Wright is a past president of the Bergen County Historical Society and of the Sussex County Historical Society and borough historian of River Edge. He has thirty years of professional experience in heritage interpretation and was central to the visioning process for the first Hackensack River Festival, the Bergen Dutch Folk Art Exhibit (1983), Historic New Bridge Landing, Lusscroft Farms in Wantage Township, the Newton Town Plot Historic District and the State History Fair at Washington Crossing. He has served as secretary to the Historic New Bridge Landing Park Commission since 1995 and as a member of the Newton Historic Preservation Advisory Commission since 1987. He frequently writes on historical subjects for 201 Magazine *and for* Bergen's Attic, *the BCHS newsletter, and co-authored a book on High Point of the Blue Mountains. Wright is author of* 1609: A Country That Was Never Lost, *published in 2009 to commemorate the 400th anniversary of Henry Hudson's visit with North Americans of the Middle Atlantic Coast. In 1985 his research brought international attention to New Jersey's claim of sovereignty over Liberty and Ellis Islands. His wife, Deborah Powell, current president of the Bergen County Historical Society, is a graphic designer and art director for a major New Jersey real estate corporation. She edits* Bergen's Attic *and designed and maintains the BCHS website.*

George Washington in Bergen County, November 1776

A Study in Leadership

William Pat Schuber

*There comes a special moment in everyone's life, a moment for which
that person was born. That special opportunity, when he seizes it, will
fulfill his mission—a mission for which he is uniquely qualified. In
that moment he finds greatness. It is his finest hour.*
—*Winston Churchill*

While the great British prime minister was referring to himself and
the British people during the dark days of World War II, his stirring
words could just as well apply to George Washington during the early days of
the American Revolution, particularly during those bleak days of November
1776 in Bergen County, New Jersey. From November 13 through November
21, Washington formed the foundations of his leadership style that would
weather the storm of the difficult challenges facing the fledgling Continental
army and nation. Implicit in my view of Washington's leadership is the
premise that leaders make a difference and that our eventual freedom from
Britain is a direct result of the leadership of one man, George Washington.

As a former government and political leader, I have always been
fascinated with the role that strong, effective leadership plays in the success
of an organization or endeavor. Now as an educator at Fairleigh Dickinson
University, I have the opportunity to teach leadership to a new generation
of students. There is no doubt in my mind that strong effective leadership
can make the difference between success or failure of any organization, be
it business, government or even a new nation. Leaders are not born but are
rather developed through a learning process over time.

Nineteenth-century image of General George Washington. *Source unknown.*

First, we should start with a definition. A review of the shelves of local bookstores showed at least one hundred titles concerning leadership, including at least two about George Washington: *George Washington on Leadership* by Richard Brookhiser and *The Ascent of George Washington* by John Ferling. It seems that everyone has his own take of what makes an effective leader. My definition of effective leadership is: the process of influencing people, groups or organizations to accomplish their goals. This definition is brief but embraces many different skills.

Leadership thus involves both rational and emotional sides of the human experience. It includes actions and influences based on reasons and logic on one hand as well as those based on inspiration and passion on the other. Thus, leadership can be looked at as both science and art.

George Washington represents a fulfillment of that definition. As the first leader of our army and nation, he had to render, through his leadership, a series of decisions for which there was no prior example. His ability to do so and to inspire a new nation was the result of the leadership lessons he acquired throughout his life. A salient time for the forging of his leadership was the significant time he spent in Bergen County in November 1776. It is the leadership of Washington during those perilous times that I wish to review in this article as a lesson of history and local pride as well as an opportunity to provide leadership examples and lessons to a wide array of Bergen County citizens.

A key method to learn leadership is to examine case studies and examples of historical leaders. I have found that one of the interesting ways to do this is to conduct a Leadership Staff Ride. This training exercise is modeled after the military staff ride used by the United States Army to train its future leaders. The staff ride was developed by the Prussian army in the mid-1800s and used by the U.S. Army in the early 1900s as a way to further the development of officers. A staff ride consists of a preliminary study and an extensive visit to the actual sites of a military campaign to examine and better understand the actions of battlefield leaders in times of stress. In such an exercise, issues such as of command and control, communication, planning, mission and decision-making are examined in context of real world events for the purpose of developing leadership principles for future leaders. Participants take on the role of historical actors, exchange and debate ideas and examine the dilemmas faced by these leaders of the past in the actual places where events unfolded.

I have used this training exercise successfully with organizations such as the New Jersey State Chiefs of Police Association and the New Jersey State Police. I have used the battlefields at Trenton, Princeton and Monmouth Courthouse as the sites to study the leadership of General Washington and a variety of British and Hessian opponents. This provides a context for a lively discussion of the different leadership styles of these historic figures and the ability to draw leadership examples and lessons for current leaders.

I believe that Bergen County during November 1776 can serve as an excellent subject for such a Leadership Staff Ride. From November 13 through November 21, 1776, the fate of the nation hung in the balance in the area from Fort Lee through Hackensack and onto the Passaic River. The experiences, actions and even the mistakes of George Washington during that time helped forge his effective leadership style, which resulted in eventual victory. The following represents a proposed Leadership Staff Ride of the key locations of that momentous time here in our county. I hope it can serve as a hands-on, low-stress training exercise for modern organizations that are developing new leadership, and as an important lesson in our history, as well as a greater appreciation and an understanding of the sacrifices made by an earlier generation, who established the freedoms that we enjoy.

LEADERSHIP STAFF RIDE
REVOLUTIONARY BERGEN COUNTY
RETREAT TO VICTORY
NOVEMBER 13–21, 1776

Site 1: Fort Lee Historic Park

A review of the actions and decisions of George Washington in and around Fort Lee provides a treasure-trove of leadership lessons.

First of all, an effective leader must establish a strategic mission and provide strategic goals to accomplish it. For Washington the mission was clear: to win freedom from Britain and to create a free and independent nation. To attain this Washington established two key strategic goals: to protect the integrity of the Continental army and to win victories against the British army and its Hessian allies. To bring his vision about, a leader needs a strategic plan and ability to communicate his ideas to superiors, peers and subordinates. These were all skills in which Washington excelled. Indeed, the creation of Fort Lee (originally Fort Constitution) in the summer of 1776 was part of that strategic plan. Its purpose, along with Fort Washington on the Manhattan side of the Hudson River, was to protect lines of communication and to prevent British incursions up the river.

In an age before radios and telephones, Washington was a master of communications. His preferred method was writing letters. Even during the most difficult times, Washington found time to communicate by letter with the Continental Congress, state governors and fellow generals. From the time he decided to cross into New Jersey from New York on November 11, until his crossing of the Passaic River on November 21, he wrote no fewer than five separate letters to the Continental Congress as well as five letters to other generals. In doing so, he kept them informed of current happenings, requested help and provided a steady hand during a time of crisis. By these actions he forged a series of important allies to help accomplish his overall goals. A good leader recognizes, no matter how skillful he is, that he cannot accomplish all of his goals without willing allies.

A good leader also must acquire good information and use it to guide decision-making. By November 8 and 9, Washington had received information from his fledgling spy network, which he had established, that the British would possibly invade New Jersey. In accordance with his proactive style of leadership he immediately made plans to cross part of his army into New Jersey to interdict any British forces. By November 13, Washington was at the headquarters of General Nathanael Greene, commander at Fort Lee, in order to judge circumstances for himself. Over the next six days, Washington would shuttle back and forth to Greene's headquarters and to Fort Lee several times, always seeking to evaluate the unfolding situations as well as to add his own personal encouragement to his subordinate officers and troops.

Despite his own feeling that Fort Washington should be abandoned, Washington delegated that authority to his key subordinate, General Greene, for whom he had great trust. He also felt that Greene had better information. Greene believed that Fort Washington should and could be defended and indeed allowed it to be reinforced. Washington never countermanded this order. By November 15, the British demanded the surrender of Fort Washington. Washington returned to Fort Lee and witnessed for himself the unfolding disaster as Colonel Robert Magaw surrendered the fort to the British with the loss of 2,800 men.

From a leadership perspective, Washington immediately knew that he had made a mistake and had to be disappointed in the actions of General Greene. However, a good leader must take responsibilities for his mistakes and must learn from them. This Washington did. In his letter to Congress on November 16, he acknowledged that he had given Greene the authority to do this. He saw no scapegoat and did not sugarcoat the bad news. A lesser leader might have blamed General Greene and fired him. Rather, Washington saw Greene's greater strengths of command and administration that would come to the fore in future years. He also appreciated his loyalty. A good leader recognizes, nurtures and rewards earned loyalty in subordinates. But Washington did learn a valuable lesson; in the future he would go with his gut and steer decisions with due consultations in the way that he wanted them.

Site 2: Huyler's Landing

The British landing at the foot of the Palisades in the late evening of November 19 represented one of the most brilliant military maneuvers of the war. Achieving tactical surprise, General Cornwallis and his five thousand troops ascended the sheer cliffs along a steep and slippery path guided by local Tories. By the late morning of November 20, the British had gained the top of the Palisades, formed into two columns and proceeded south with the intent of capturing Fort Lee.

While this remarkable action represented significant British success and pending disaster for Washington, the leadership lesson in this instance shows just the opposite: Washington was at his very best under great pressure while the British leadership displayed its imperial arrogance.

Washington heard of the invasion in the early morning of November 20 at his headquarters in Hackensack and reacted immediately and decisively. He did not panic but immediately dispatched orders to General Greene to abandon Fort Lee with his troops. Then in an act of great courage, so typical of Washington, he proceeded out personally to meet the retreating army.

A good leader must be flexible in his planning. It's important for leaders to remember that it is very rare for any plan not to require any changes upon implementation. A German military saying states that no battle plan survives its first contact with the enemy. Washington initially indicated that he was prepared to fight the British, but upon learning of their great numbers, he wisely changed his plans to extricate his army across the Hackensack River in order to prevent its capture. Washington had skillfully shown the ability to adapt to turbulent changing circumstances.

On the other hand, British leadership missed a great opportunity to potentially end the war on this day. Despite the fact Cornwallis's advanced guard skirmished with elements of Greene's retreating troops, Cornwallis refused to reinforce them. He had been given an order to capture Fort Lee and this was what he did. I do not believe Cornwallis sought to bring about an engagement; rather, his contempt for the abilities of the Continental soldier caused him to believe that they would be defeated in due time. While he captured supplies he had also captured an empty fort, for Greene's army made good its escape. Many have argued that Cornwallis's actions were in keeping with his orders from General Howe and in fact they were. However, there was a certain arrogance exhibited there with the British. It was implicit in their actions that the capture of geography was more important than the capture of Washington's army. In fact Washington's army would escape to fight again.

Site 3: Liberty Pole
(Corner of Lafayette and Palisade Avenues, Englewood)

Historic marker at Liberty Pole, Englewood. *Courtesy of Ira Lieblich.*

It was near Liberty Pole that advance elements of Captain Johann Ewald and his Hessian Jägers first spotted "the glitter of bayonets and the cloud of dust" of the Fort Lee garrison. Skirmishing broke out and Captain Ewald communicated with General Cornwallis to seek reinforcements. General Cornwallis purportedly said, "Let them go, my dear Ewald, and stay here. We do not want to lose any men. One Jäger is worth more than 10 rebels." While the British army and its leaders represented the peak of military professionalism, that very professionalism bred arrogance and complacency that caused the British to severely underestimate Washington and his army's abilities. This was a mistake that the British repeated to their misfortune. A key leadership lesson here is to never, ever underestimate your competitor and to follow through completely on the opportunities that you have gained.

On the other hand, Washington knew that he had to act immediately. Time was not on his side and his personal intervention was necessary. It was at Liberty Pole that Washington rallied Greene's troops and led them personally to the strategic crossing of the Hackensack River at New Bridge Landing. As a leadership lesson, we see the importance as Washington did, that his personal presence was very important in steadying the potential panic of his troops by sharing their danger. In essence he provided a great leadership lesson of leading from the front.

General Washington became a symbol of strength at a time of great turmoil. As a leader, never underestimate the power of your personal presence to inspire. If Washington had not shown decisive leadership and made himself visible frequently to his troops, one wonders what the outcome might have been.

Site 4: New Bridge Landing—River Edge

This location represented the key strategic crossing of the Hackensack River at that time. It was essential for Washington to cross his troops here to place this river between them and the British. Here we see Washington exhibiting another important leadership skill: the management of time. Washington knew he had little time to wait and used all his strengths to hurry his retreating forces to this strategic crossing. Again, he did this through his personal examples of riding forth and urging on his troops. He exhibited a key leadership principle of leading from the front. On the other hand, General Cornwallis and his army showed no sense of urgency. Hence, Washington escaped and the chance to end the war was lost.

By November 21, light infantry and Jägers had come up to New Bridge. Washington had posted his rear guard and a fight broke out on the bridge. Cornwallis's troops discovered that Washington's men could defend themselves very well and did not act as a defeated army.

The leadership lesson here is that a leader must always take advantage of his assets and environment. Here Washington skillfully used the natural contours of the river to block the British with a well-placed defensive force. The second leadership lesson is to never lose hope, even in the most difficult of circumstances. Washington had inculcated this message upon his rear guard and they performed with great courage.

Colonials Retreating Past Von Steuben House. Illustration by permission of Gray's Watercolors, grayswatercolors@rcn.com.

Zabriskie House. Illustration by permission of Gray's Watercolors, grayswatercolors@rcn.com.

Site 5: The Hackensack Green

On November 13, Washington had arrived here from New York with all expectation of stopping the British. He made his headquarters in the Mansion House of Peter Zabriskie, which stood at the northeast corner of Main Street and Washington Place. Now on November 20, his troops arrived in Hackensack after escaping from Fort Lee. It was a cold and rainy night, and the Americans were discouraged. They spent the night camped along Main Street and near the Green. A lesser person might have despaired and sought to save himself rather than look out for the organization. This was not George Washington. Coolly and calmly he adjusted his plans and ordered a retreat to the Passaic River and dispatched the rear guard to New Bridge Landing. The vigor of their defense and the success of the retreat is a tribute to Washington's calm and inspirational leadership. The leadership lesson here is to never let the enemy—or your colleagues—see you sweat.

Site 6: Acquackanonk Bridge
(Corner of Main and Passaic Streets, Wallington)

Washington's army proceeded down Main Street to Polifly Road and then onto the Passaic River crossing at Acquackanonk. As the commander, Washington could have been the first to cross the river, but he chose to ride in the rear of the column, thereby sharing the danger with his troops. A good leader never asks his subordinates to undertake a task or risk anything that he would not do himself. By sharing his soldiers' dangers, Washington exhibited the important leadership quality of empathy. Here a leader undertakes to bear the same hardships as his troops.

Future President James Monroe, then a Virginia lieutenant, was part of this column. He later wrote, "I saw him [Washington] at the head of a small band, or rather in its rear, for he was always near the enemy and his countenance and manner made an impression on me which I never forgot."

By the evening of November 21, Washington's army had crossed the Passaic River intact. It would live again to fight another day.

I am sure that as the retreat continued Washington was formulating plans to turn this desperate situation into a positive opportunity. He would watch and wait for an opportunity to strike an unexpected blow against the British foe. A good leader always exhibits hope, seeks opportunity in adversity and never fails to inspire a vision of success. For Washington and the Continental army, Christmas was coming and a little town called Trenton loomed over the horizon. A glimmer of a new plan was taking shape. But that is the story for another staff ride and another chapter in New Jersey history.

CONCLUSION

It was in Bergen County that George Washington emerged as a true leader. Washington was not perfect; he made mistakes and was still learning. But a good leader learns from his mistakes. One does not have to be a national leader to emulate the leadership lessons exhibited in the foregoing staff ride. I hope that the leaders, directors and personnel of all kinds of organizations in Bergen County and beyond will undertake this Leadership Staff Ride and see it as an opportunity to train new leaders in their organization, to reinvigorate their employees and to gain a greater appreciation of our historical heritage. George Washington remains a powerful symbol of selfless leadership that transcends the centuries. He is more than a marble statue or a face on our currency; he is the very reason that we exist as a nation.

William "Pat" Schuber, Esq., is a senior lecturer at the School of Administrative Science, Petrocelli College, Fairleigh Dickinson University. He is a faculty member in the Master of Administrative Science (MAS), Master of Science in Homeland Security (MSHS), Master of Sports Administration (MSA) and Bachelor of Arts in Individualized Studies (BAIS). His subjects include leadership, government, law, ethics and communication. Pat has conducted Leadership Staff Ride Seminars at Gettysburg Battlefield, Antietam Battlefield, Trenton, Princeton Battlefield and Normandy, France. He lectures frequently on military history, historical leadership, ethics, communication and conflict resolution to numerous civic groups. He has written several scholarly articles and co-authored books on topics of history, leadership and homeland security. He served as the county executive of Bergen County for twelve years, nine years as a member of the New Jersey State Assembly and mayor of the Borough of Bogota for four years. He served as a captain in the U.S. Army Reserve (Retired). Pat is a graduate of Fordham University with a BA and received his JD at Fordham University School of Law

The Reverend Gerrit Lydekker:
From Coetus to Conferentie

An Explanation of "What Happened"

Firth Haring Fabend

Of the forty-one Reformed Dutch ministers in New York and New Jersey at the time of the Revolution, only four were Tories. A look at the career of one of them, the Reverend Gerrit Lydekker, Tory pastor of the Reformed Dutch Church in English Neighborhood (today's Cliffside Park / Fairview / Fort Lee / Leonia / Palisades Park / Ridgefield / southern Englewood), sheds light on what would eventually amount, especially in Bergen County, to a civil war within the War of Revolution, for his career encompasses all the issues that roiled the Reformed Church and the citizens of Bergen County in the decades from the 1730s through the Revolution.

On the eve of the eve of the Revolution, the Reverend Classis of Amsterdam in the Province of North Holland, which had oversight of the Reformed Dutch churches in New York and New Jersey, wrote a scolding twenty-three-page letter to them, washing their hands of the churches' long-drawn-out bickering behavior. "We shall no more in the future treat with you," their High Mightinesses fumed in high dungeon. It was June 3, 1765. The Stamp Act had recently been proclaimed by Parliament, and Patrick Henry had just introduced resolutions asserting that the House of Burgesses possessed the "only and sole and exclusive right and power to lay taxes" on Virginians. In fact, Parliament, he asserted, had no legal authority to tax the colonies at all, an opinion held by many New Jersey inhabitants as well. The New Jersey Committee of Correspondence had put it this way in September 1764: "We look upon all Taxes laid upon us without our Consent as a fundamental infringement of the Rights and privileges Secured to us as English Subjects."

But it was not taxes the churches bickered about. A few months earlier, on February 4, 1765, the Classis had written to the churches that "it was a

Historic marker on Hillside Avenue, Leonia. *Courtesy of Ira Lieblich.*

matter of grief" to it, "that, although all the brethren assembled together, both of the Conferentie and of the Coetus, the latter soon withdrew [June 20, 1764] on account of certain considerations which they thought ought first be referred to [us]. Thus all our efforts and labors, and the former resolutions and acts of approval of both the Classis and the Synod, have resulted in nothing whatever."

The efforts the Classis referred to were its attempts to reconcile two hostile factions within the Dutch Reformed Church in New York and New Jersey, the Coetus, a term for assembly, and the Conferentie, meaning conference. The original Coetus, unified but toothless, had been organized in 1738, at the suggestion of the Classis of Amsterdam, for the purpose of clergymen and their elders meeting annually and "agreeing together" on local issues as they arose. The Coetus, which did not actually meet until 1747, reorganized in 1754 in the hopes of eventually becoming an independent classis that would have all the rights of the Classis of Amsterdam—that is, be equal to it within the Synod of North Holland. But the conservatives within the Coetus soon repudiated this move toward independence, and the more liberal ministers and their elders eventually withdrew from the body, wanting true autonomy, not mere permission to meet and agree together on local issues.

The issue of independence versus subordination was paramount, but other issues that convulsed the two factions were the Coetus's desire to educate the clergy in an academy or seminary established on American soil, to license candidates for the ministry and to ordain clergy in America. The Conferentie strenuously objected to these aspirations, even though as members of the original Coetus, they had already, beginning in 1741, voted to license and ordain five ministers. To further complicate matters, especially in eighteenth-century Bergen County, some Reformed ministers and congregants wanted "heart" religion, Pietist preaching, spontaneous prayer from the pulpit and less formality in general, while the more conservative ministers and congregants found ideas like the "New Birth," spiritual regeneration and deviation from Dutch traditions repugnant. Adrian Leiby has covered the coetus/conferentie topic in detail in his book *The United Churches of Hackensack and Schraalenburgh*, and a forthcoming doctoral dissertation by Dirk Mouw of the University of Iowa goes into even greater detail.

All of these issues were exacerbated in the run-up to the War of Revolution, as the desire for "independency" within the Dutch Reformed Church, and thus within all those communities in New York and New Jersey where the Church was the primary cultural institution, mirrored the political desire of colonists to be free of Great Britain's rule. Patriots were motivated by a horror of losing their liberty to the tyranny of an "enslaving" king and Parliament, and Patriot churchgoers and clergy could easily see a like tyranny in the Classis of Amsterdam's insistence on maintaining control of the colonial church. But also within the same communities and the same church, the Divine Right of Kings was remembered, and for Tory churchgoers and clergy the horror was to dishonor the king. For them, a break from Great Britain was an affront to the rule of law and to God, who had ordained, they believed, that the governance of the colonies belonged to the Monarch and his Parliament, with men duty bound to defer and obey. Feelings eventually ran so high that the Coetus/Conferentie conflict evolved into a virtual civil war within the War of Revolution, with families and former friends and neighbors pitted against one another. Violence was endemic. It is well described in another work by Adrian Leiby, *The Revolutionary War in the Hackensack Valley*, and in my fictional treatment of the conflict, *Land So Fair*.

The final straw that caused the Classis of Amsterdam in June 1765 to denounce the Dutch churches in New York and New Jersey was a five-year-long series of exchanges between Domine Johannes Leydt of the Coetus and Domine Johannes Ritzema of the Conferentie over Leydt's pamphlet "True Liberty the Way to Peace." This pamphlet, which Leydt had published in August 1760, was addressed to the "Reverend Consistories of all the Dutch Reformed Churches in our Country." The peace to which he refers is the end of hostilities between Coetus and Conferentie. "I deem it to be my duty, and yours also," Leydt wrote, "to labor with such earnest zeal, that we (for the conservation of the liberty and the rights of the church of God) may attain unto a peaceful and a General union." Leydt's object was for full unanimity not only on the reunion question, but also on the overriding question of subordination versus independence, and the lesser but still vexing ones of local licensing and ordination.

A look at the career of Gerrit Lydekker (his preferred spelling; it is also often spelled Garret Leydecker) will shed light on the issues that underlay the Coetus-Conferentie conflict and that complicated the course of the Revolution as it unfolded in Bergen County.

Gerrit Lydekker first appears in the church records in 1755. A "J. Leydecker, elder," attended the Coetus meeting in New York during the week of October 7–12, 1755, with Domine John H. Goetschius, minister of the United Churches of Hackensack and Schraalenburgh. The "J" is a mistake for "G," for the Schraalenburgh church records indicate that G. Lydekker, age twenty-six in 1755 and a recent graduate of the College of New Jersey (Princeton), was an elder that year. He was elected to this office without first having served as a deacon, the usual course, which indicates a high regard by church leaders for his religious "walk." The records indicate that he served two two-year terms until 1759 and then one more two-year term from 1762 to 1764. There would have been no objection to his serving a second two-year term at this point, but he did not. Why not?

Domine Goetschius (himself ordained on American soil by the Coetus in 1741) was a fervent Pietist, or New Lighter, and was to become a notable Patriot in the war. For Gerrit Lydekker, fresh out of Princeton, to have been his elder for six years between 1755 and 1764 suggests that Lydekker was also a Pietist, a follower of the Great Awakening, which had informed the founding of Princeton in 1746, and where Lydekker would, of course, have imbibed Awakening ideas, style and rhetoric.

Further support for his Pietism is found in "A Discourse on the Greatness, and Praise of the Lord," composed and delivered by Gerrit Lydekker, AB, and published in New York in 1766. It is a work that reveals no aversion to evangelical language or doctrine. Its message is "Be ye perfect" in order to inherit the kingdom. "Let all impenitent Sinners fly to Christ with the wings of an unfeigned Faith and with deep Repentence," Gerrit wrote. A long paean praising the perfection, omniscience and omnipotence of God and urging its readers to study God's "two grand Volumes, or Books, namely the great Book of Nature and the greater supernatural Book of Grace, or the holy Bible," Lydekker's Discourse is entirely within the conventional Awakening rhetoric of the day.

If serving as elder with Goetschius and his published "Discourse" are not conclusive evidence of Lydekker's progressive and Pietist mindset in the 1750s, another clue to his loyalties may be that just one year before he first became an elder, September 17–19, 1754, Domine Johannes Ritzema and Domine Samuel Verbryck, respectively president and scribe of the then still-unified (but still ineffectual) Coetus, had recommended to Amsterdam that the American Dutch Reformed churches be allowed to establish their own long-desired classis on American soil. In doing so, they were simply conveying to their High Mightinesses what had been a unanimous decision by the Coetus.

The Coetus made this momentous decision to ask for an American classis just as the controversy over the founding of King's College (Columbia) by a group of Episcopalian ministers was bursting onto the scene. The Reformed Dutch grew mightily opposed to this plan, fearing that the proposed new college would be too closely affiliated with the Church of England and would be dominated by Anglican clerics and Royal officials, who would likely try to establish an Anglican episcopacy in America. This was an unpalatable idea to the Dutch Reformed Church, which still remembered its own days as the "official" public church of New Netherland. The church recalled its guarantee of autonomy by the Articles of Capitulation in 1664, and its incorporation by the Crown in 1696 with continuing guarantees of the Dutch right to private liberty of conscience and the right to worship publicly according to the church's own customs and rules of church discipline.

However, in an unforeseen outcome, a month after signing this letter recommending the establishment of an American classis, Domine Ritzema, who entertained hopes of being appointed a professor in the aborning Episcopalian college, inexplicably changed his mind on the subject.

The Coetus, enraged at Ritzema's change of face and lack of loyalty, demanded at its meeting the following year (October 7–14, 1755) that he turn over their Minute Book, correspondence with Amsterdam, other papers belonging to the Coetus and the treasurer's records, and this order was agreed to "without a dissenting vote." In other words, in October 1755, Gerrit Lydekker, who was present as Goetschius's elder, voted with everyone else to agree that Ritzema must return the Coetus records to the Coetus. We should take this to be evidence that Lydekker was pro-Coetus and a supporter of Goetschius in October 1755.

In the interim, however, had come a new development. Six months before, in April 1755, the Reverend Theodorus J. Frelinghuysen Jr. called the Reformed Dutch ministers and consistories together "to take measures for seeking the establishment of a Classis and founding an Academy." This meeting was held in New York City in May 1755, and it authorized Frelinghuysen—in a direct rebuff to Ritzema's academic ambitions regarding King's College—to go to Holland to seek funds "for a University for the Dutch Church."

Ritzema, now thoroughly irked, pronounced the May 1755 meeting illegal and flatly refused to turn over the Coetus records. For the next nine years his correspondence, published in the *Ecclesiastical Records of the State of New York*, is involved primarily with four interrelated issues: the King's College matter, Leydt's pamphlets, the desire for English preaching in the New York Dutch churches and the tendency of the Dutch churches to "independency." Although he favored English preaching, Ritzema deeply feared the outcome of an independent Dutch Reformed Church with its own classis in America, especially one whose clergy were "given up to fanaticism" and "so-called 'preaching the spirit.'"

Things came to a head at the aforementioned session of the Coetus on June 20, 1764, when the Coetus, dissatisfied with Amsterdam's longtime recalcitrance on the classis question, withdrew from the meeting, at which point the Conferentie organized itself as "The Assembly Subordinate to the Reverend Classis," complete with elders. That same day, Gerrit Lydekker appeared before the newly organized group to request it to write on his behalf to the Classis of Amsterdam for permission to admit him to the qualifying examination to become a candidate for the ministry.

If Gerrit Lydekker was of a progressive and Pietist bent and an elder of the Pietist Goetschius from 1755 until 1764, what caused him in June 1764 to become a public supporter of the Conferentie faction, now headed by the conservative Ritzema? As Adrian Leiby put it, "something happened." What was it that happened to turn Lydekker away from his one-time tutor and longtime minister Goetschius and to ally himself with Ritzema? The answer will become clear.

The day after his request for examination, the Conferentie duly wrote to the Classis of Amsterdam to recommend that they be allowed to examine Gerrit Lydekker as a candidate for the ministry. They praised him "in the strongest terms" as having been taught from his youth in Latin and Greek, for having studied for four years at the College of New Jersey (Princeton), after which he spent a year and a half studying divinity first under Goetschius (as we know from another source, they do not mention it) and then under Domine Ritzema, and in Hebrew under Domine Kals.

They described him as "a student in theology" who had a "true desire to edify his neighbors." By this they meant student in the first Oxford English Dictionary definition of the word as "a person who is in engaged in or addicted to study," not that Gerrit, now age thirty-five, was still in school. But a frail constitution ("weakness of body") had always kept him from undertaking the voyage to Holland for ordination, they wrote, and "being convinced that the irregular ordination by the Coetus ministers was inconsistent with our [Reformed Church] constitution, he has never been able to unite with them. So he has spent six or seven years without any prospect" of a pulpit, they concluded. (The six or seven years would date back to 1757, which would account for the eighteen months he spent studying with Ritzema and Kals after graduation from Princeton in 1755.)

Six months later, the Classis gave its permission for the "well-educated young gentleman" to be ordained in New Jersey (February 4, 1765), and the Conferentie, after some years opposing local ordination, did an abrupt about face and, "knowing him to be properly qualified," ordained the man.

These extraordinary developments took place in the midst of the five-year back-and-forth arguments running anywhere from 20 to 120 pages between Leydt and Ritzema that had so exasperated the Classis of Amsterdam in 1765 that it finally washed its hands of the warring factions.

As we have seen, one of these arguments was the right of the Coetus to license and ordain clergy. But if the Conferentie was apparently not opposed to local ordination after all, having undertaken to ordain Lydekker, what was the real issue that had motivated its members to separate themselves from the Coetus in June 1764? And how did this relate to Lydekker's not staying on for a routine follow-up term, which could easily have been his, to his 1762 eldership in Goetschius's church? Either the office was not offered to him again, or he refused it. And what did it have to do with Lydekker's conversion to the Conferentie?

Perhaps Lydekker's change of heart had to do with sides taken in the King's College controversy, which still raged in 1764, and of which his mentor Ritzema was in the thick, or in the language controversy that convulsed the Reformed Church at the arrival in the early winter of 1764 of the Reverend Archibald Laidlie to preach in English in the New York Dutch Reformed congregations. (Although Ritzema favored English preaching, many in the city and in Bergen County opposed it.) But perhaps it had most to do with the long-simmering subordination versus

Historic image of Reverend Gerrit Lydekker. *Courtesy of the Seeley G. Mudd Manuscript Library, Princeton University, Princeton, New Jersey.*

independency issue, which convulsed the Classis of Amsterdam particularly in 1763, as ample correspondence shows, and which was also finding resonance in the Revolutionary rhetoric beginning to be heard at this time.

For example, in a letter to the Coetus on January 11, 1763, the Classis wrote: "Brethren, consider what will be the result of your withdrawal from the Netherlands Church? Will it not be the beginning of the introduction of 'British' tyranny in the Church?...Would you not be the instrumentality of having your 'Dutch Church' liberties assailed, which you have enjoyed (from the English conquest) until now?...Try to prevent those bad results, which will confuse or completely destroy your congregations, by uniting together again in a Coetus subordinate to the Classis of Amsterdam."

There is one shred of direct evidence to suggest that the best explanation for Gerrit Lydekker's switch in allegiance from Coetus to Conferentie in 1764 and from thence to Toryism was his conviction that, as the Classis of Amsterdam was the legal and lawful authority over the American churches, so the King of England was the legal and lawful authority over the American colonies. In neither case was independence an option for Gerrit.

We have few direct words of Gerrit Lydekker to lead us to his most basic beliefs, much less to an explanation for his embrace of the conservative Conferentie ideology in 1764 and the Tory side in the war in 1776. But just as his highly pious "Discourse" of 1766 tells us that he was a New Light in his religious leanings, so an obscure footnote that he inserted in his only other known publication gives a clue as to his political views.

This 1787 publication is his translation from the "low Dutch" of "A Treatise, in answer to the Proposed Question, What Arguments do Nature and Reason afford for the Existence of God; how far may we know this Being; and what moral Consequences can be deduced from it?" The author was the Reverend Petrus Schouten. In the chapter starting on page 133, "Concerning the Love to the Public," the Reverend Schouten asserts, "If you reverence, honor and obey the Magistrates, and circumspectly refrain from all that may disturb the peace; [and] earnestly pursue your calling [etc.],...will you not then also do as much for the Gen. Welfare, or Good of the Public?"

Immediately after the phrase "If you reverence, honor and obey the Magistrates," Gerrit inserted his gratuitous footnote.

If it seems not only presumptuous but also rather arrogant of Lydekker to have interjected his opinions in another man's treatise at the mention of honoring and obeying the magistrates, i.e., the civil authorities, then let us take a look at this curious interruption in Schouten's Treatise to see what to make of it. The footnote occurs on page 135. It reads: "In proof and confirmation of the doctrine here advanced by our great and learned Author [Schouten], Vis. that we ought to be good and loyal subjects, I shall adduce the subsequent arguments [for this doctrine] from the sacred Scriptures."

Here he cites Romans 13:1–7, Ecclesiastes 10:20, Exodus 22:28, Proverbs 19:12 and Matthew 22:15–21. The relevant phrases are, respectively, from Romans: "Let every person be subject to the governing authorities [as]... instituted by God...for the authorities are ministers of God."

From Ecclesiastes: "Even in your thought, do not curse the king."

From Exodus: "You shall not revile God, nor curse a ruler of your people."

From Proverbs: "A king's wrath is like the growling of a lion."

And from Matthew: "Render unto Caesar the things that are Caesar's, and to God the things that are God's."

Finally, he cites the "sacred Injunction of St. Peter, in his First Epistle, chap. ii.13–17," which he quotes verbatim from the King James Version of the Bible:

> *13. Submit yourselves to every ordinance of man, for the Lord's sake: whether it be to the King, as Supreme;*
>
> *14. Or unto Governors, as unto them that are sent by him for the punishment of evil doers, and for the praise of them that do Well.*
>
> *15. For so is the Will of God, that with well-doing ye put to silence the ignorance of foolish men:*
>
> *16. As free, and not using your liberty for a cloak of maliciousness, but as the servants of God.*
>
> *17. Honour all men. Love the brotherhood. Fear God. Honour the King.*

He concludes: "That we may one and all be induced to love, fear and obey, the amiable the tremendous God, and honour the King, and receive eternal, perfect felicity, which is the sure, great, and most gracious reward of keeping the Divine Commandments, is the sincere wish, and most earnest prayer of THE TRANSLATOR."

We have to conclude that Gerrit Lydekker—no doubt influenced by the acrimonious arguments in the Leydt/Ritzema pamphlet war and the outrage of the Classis of Amsterdam at being "abused," "scorned" and "slandered" by the Coetus ministers, who had approved Leydt's publications—had espoused the intellectual argument that God's earthly authorities were not to be defied. In other words, it was not presumption or arrogance that led Leydekker to insert his views on civil obedience in Schouten's treatise, but rather the "true desire" of this "well-educated gentleman preacher" and "student of theology" to edify his readers, a desire so strong that it overwhelmed and superseded the customary self-effacing role of translator. Even four years after the end of the Revolution, apparently, he remained convinced that the King of England had been the rightful ruler of the American colonies, just as the Classis of Amsterdam had been the rightful authority of the American Dutch Reformed churches.

Some accounts of Lydekker's career prior to the Revolution say that he was "called" to the North Branch Reformed Church in 1767. But this church "removed to Readington" in 1738, and the published history of the Readington Reformed Church makes no mention of any Lydekker or Leydecker among its ministers. The Reverend Dr. Jacob Rutsen Hardenbergh, a fervent Pietist and later Patriot, was in the Readington pulpit during these years—years that were colored by a deep split in the congregation between "Coetus men" and those favoring subordination, known as the Malcontents. The conclusion is inescapable that, at most, Lydekker ministered to the Malcontents within the congregation, not to the main body, and according to Corwin's *Manual*, only in 1767.

In 1770 Lydekker was called to the newly formed church at English

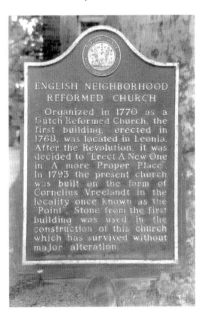

Historic marker for the English Neighborhood Reformed Church, Ridgefield. *Courtesy of Ira Lieblich.*

Neighborhood, and here he remained until 1776, the year that found him praying for the king and the royal family from the pulpit in disobedience of the express dictate of the Congress, which had stated that to do so was an act of treason. Again, his loyalties to the king as God's deputy on earth were so strong, his principles so founded in Holy Writ, that he defied the new American authorities and risked his property if not his life in their defense.

When the war broke out, Lydekker fled Bergen County for British-held New York City, where he was granted the use of St. George's Chapel at Trinity Church (Episcopal) and where he ministered to the Dutch Loyalists in the city for the duration of the war. Meanwhile, Bergen County Patriots looted his home, and the authorities seized his farm of four

English Neighborhood Reformed Church, Ridgefield. *Courtesy of Ira Lieblich.*

hundred acres, plus another parcel of ten acres. He testified later that his losses amounted to £2,523/6.8. After the war, when he resettled in England, the British government compensated him for approximately half of this amount and gave him a small annuity.

In sum, in the Revolution, Gerrit Lydekker, Bergen County Tory and Reformed Dutch minister, made a decision to remain loyal to King George III, in his own words to "honour the King" as his civil authority, in the same way that he honored the Classis of Amsterdam as his ecclesiastical authority. For his political views, though they were based on his interpretations of Holy Scripture, he was denounced as a traitor and suffered the loss of his real property in Bergen County, and when the British lost the war, he had to flee his native land, where his ancestors had settled nearly 150 years before. He was a man of principle and committed to his deepest beliefs about authority and order. But, probably in anger at his treatment by Patriots and the loss of his worldly goods, when he fled to New York City he took away with him the records of his congregation at English Neighborhood, which have never resurfaced.

He is perhaps better remembered today among Bergen County historians and genealogists for that act of retaliation than for his reasons for honoring his king.

————•————

Firth Haring Fabend is an independent historian with a doctorate in American studies from New York University. She is the author of the prizewinning works A Dutch Family in the Middle Colonies, 1660–1800 *and* Zion on the Hudson: Dutch New York and New Jersey in the Age of Revivals, *both published by Rutgers University Press. She has also published many essays on the Dutch Colonial experience and most recently a historical novel,* Land So Fair, *set in the Hudson Valley in the eighteenth century. She is a Fellow of the New Netherland Project, the Holland Society of New York and the New York Academy of History.*

THE 1779 CLOSTER
LANDING RAIDS

ERIC NELSEN

In the middle of Everett Road, a quiet side street in Demarest, on an island ringed by evergreen bushes, is the "Sauches Taves Begraven Ground." Among the several dozen stones in this curious little graveyard, one stands out from the others:

> *Here lie*
> *the Remains of*
> *DOUWE TALEMA*
> *Who died on the 11. Day of May, 1779*
> *in his Ninetieth Year.*
> *This aged Man at his Residence*
> *near this Place was willfully and*
> *barbarously murdered by a Party*
> *of Tories, Traitors to their Country*
> *who had taken Refuge with the Troops*
> *of Britain then in New York and came*
> *thence to murder, burn and plunder.*

I remember coming upon the graveyard and reading that stone as a teenager while out exploring on my bicycle—and being amazed: this happened in Demarest, New Jersey? Many years later, my research into the Kearney House, along the shore of the Hudson at what was called the Closter Dock, brought me back to this gravestone to take a closer look at the story it tells.

The wound that ended the life of Douwe Tallman (as his surname is usually written today) was from a bayonet, and it was inflicted two days

Original headstone at grave site of Douwe Talema in Sauches Taves Begraven Ground, Demarest. *Courtesy of Ira Lieblich.*

before he succumbed to it: on May 9, 1779. It was a Sunday. The incident was part of a bitter conflict between neighbors and former neighbors that tore through what was then called "Closter," the patchwork of farms and woodlands south of Tappan and west of the Palisades, from 1776 until the end of the Revolution.

In the years just before the Revolution, the farmers of Closter built a pair of roads through natural breaks, or mountain passes, in the cliffs of the Palisades in order to construct farm landings on the Hudson River. Though steep and rugged, these roads provided the farmers with a direct route to the river and so to New York City and its markets: by hitching their teams to wooden sleds instead of wagons, the surplus of their farms could be dragged over the rough terrain and down to the shore. The crews of the sloops that tied up at the landings could then sail the farm goods to the city, thirty tons or more at a time. The farmer might make the voyage with his goods, or he might instead choose to send a son or a hired hand—or a trusted slave—to serve as his agent in the city. If correctly planned with the ebb tide, the trip from farm to city could be done in a single day. The landings were a mile and a half apart on the river, in line of sight from one another: the northern landing was called the Closter Dock, or Upper Closter Landing; the southern landing was called the New Dock, or Lower Closter Landing.

The landings' proximity and similar names led to some historical confusion over the years, but it is widely accepted today that the Lower Landing was the one used by the British forces under General Cornwallis in November 1776 for his attack on Fort Lee. Five thousand British and Hessian soldiers marched through Closter that day—and for the families who lived in Closter, the world would never be the same.

In the aftermath of that dramatic autumn and winter, many of Bergen County's Loyalist families took refuge in New York City, which remained occupied by the British for the duration of the war. This seems to have been particularly true for the Loyalists of Closter, with its relatively sparse population spread across farms that were for the most part only a generation or two removed from the swamps and woods that surrounded them. In the crowded squalor of occupied New York City, the memory of the farms they had toiled over and the tidy farmhouses that they left behind must have been a powerful impetus for many a Loyalist to take up arms for the Crown forces. They called themselves "Refugees." Some Refugees readily volunteered to return to their former neighborhoods for missions that the commanders of the regular British forces shunned.

Also seeking refuge in New York City were escaped slaves, men and women who had risked their lives for the British offer of freedom to any Rebel's slave who could make it over to their lines. Some of these men, too, no doubt felt they had good reason to return to places like Closter—places where they may have been born and come of age in bondage—but now armed, and in the company of other armed men.

The men and women who stayed in Closter, on the other hand, tended to be those who sided with the Rebel cause (along with those slaves unwilling or unable to escape to the British lines). Many of the men who stayed formed militia units, in large part to guard against their recent neighbors, Refugees, who came into Closter to drive off cattle and horses, even to attempt to take prisoners to British-held New York. The Refugee attacks often made use of the farm landings that had been recently built by the now fractured community.

The May 9 attack came through the Lower Landing, the New Dock.

As might be expected (and to use some understatement), accounts of the day's events differed between Loyalist and Rebel newspapers. Both accounts that follow were printed on Wednesday, May 12, 1779, and so were probably written after the raid but before Douwe Tallman's death.

From the Rebel *New Jersey Gazette*:

> *Extract of a letter from Closter, Bergen county, dated May 10, 1779*
> *This day* [sic: May 9] *about 100 of the enemy came by the way of New-Dock, attacked the place* [Closter], *carried off Cornelius Tallman, Samuel Demarest, Jacob Cole, and George Buskirk; killed Cornelius Demarest; wounded Henderick Demarest, Jeremiah Vestervelt* [Westervelt] *and Dow Tallman, &c. They burnt the dwelling-house[s] of Peter Demarest, Matthias Bogart, Cornelius Huyler, Samuel Demarest's house and barn, John Banta's house and barn, and Cornelius Bogart and John Vestervelt's barns. They attempted to burn every building*

they entered, but the fire was in some places extinguished. They destroyed all the furniture, &c., in many houses, and abused many of the women. In their retreat they were so closely pursued by the militia and a few continental troops, that they took off no cattle.

They were of Buskirk's corps, some of our Closter and Tappan old neighbours, joined by a party of negroes. I should have mentioned the negroes first in order to grace the British arms.

From the Loyalist *Royal Gazette*:

On Sunday morning last, a party of refugees went from New-York, in boats to Closter, a settlement abounding with many violent rebels, and persecutors of loyal subjects, and who were almost daily affording some fresh instance of barbarity. The party on their approach to their settlement, being fired upon by the militia from houses, were obliged to lay them in ashes, and after pursuing the runaways, killing five or six [and] wounding many, and bringing in four prisoners, returned to this city, having one man slightly wounded from a random shot on reembarking. On the party's first arrival at Closter they found affixed on several houses, printed papers, with the following.

"No Quarters should be given to Refugees, etc."

Some time since Mr. Myers, an Ensign in a company of refugees, was killed in a skirmish with a party of rebels near Closter, the inhabitants of that place after his death, stripp'd his corpse naked, hung him up by the neck, where he was exhibited as a public spectacle for many hours.

The inhabitants of Closter have been remarkable for their persecution of, and cruelty to all the friends of government, and had fixed up in many of their houses advertisements, in which they expressed their determination of giving no quarter to refugees, and requested all Continental soldiers and militia to refuse them quarters.

When the refugees in their late excursion entered into the village of Closter they were fired at out of the houses and barns, &c.

Both accounts agreed that the raiders came from New York City and traveled to Closter by the Hudson River. The sailing vessels that transported them would almost certainly not have begun up the river until after the flood tide began to flow at New York; modern-day tide-prediction programs indicate that this would have been shortly before noon at the Battery on May 9, 1779. It would have taken several hours to travel the seventeen miles to

The remnants of the New Dock, later called Huyler's Landing, at low tide. (Yonkers is across the Hudson River.) *Courtesy of Anthony G. Taranto Jr.*

the New Dock, where the tide would crest at around five that afternoon (the raiders would have wanted to begin their return downriver within an hour or two after that mark, to take advantage of the ebb tide).

The New Dock where they disembarked is today just a remnant. The underlying stones of what was once a substantial jetty all but disappear twice each day for an hour or two around high tide. (This was a working dock—complete with wooden decking over the stones—which remained in use by the Palisades Interstate Park through the 1930s; more than half a century of the river acting upon it, without any kind of maintenance, has reduced it to ruin.) The road along which the farmers of Closter dragged their farm goods to the river is now a hiking trail connecting the riverfront with the cliff top; the Refugees who landed that day ascended this road to the summit of the Palisades, emerging into the afternoon sun near the present-day Alpine-Tenafly border. They followed the road down the western back-slope of the Palisades ridge, through what is now a development of imposing new houses, some still under construction, on what were the links and fairways of the former Tammybrook Country Club. This area would have comprised mostly wood lots in 1779. Then as now, the Watchung Mountains would have been visible to the west as the raiders headed down the hill—and into Closter. At the bottom of the slope the road ended at its junction with the north–south County Road, near present-day downtown Cresskill. They turned right, to head north on the County Road, which still roughly follows its eighteenth-century path. Here they would have come upon the first houses, probably houses owned by the Westervelt family (though built after the Revolution, a Dutch-style Westervelt house still stands at one of the family's old homesites, just north of the Dunroven nursing home).

By both newspapers' accounts, the violence that ensued that day was exceptional, even for Closter. The raiders—one hundred armed men, according to the Rebel account—continued up the County Road that Sunday afternoon, into what is now Demarest, moving from farm to farm, attacking and burning house after house, barn after barn. Among the farms they fell upon was that of Samuel Demarest, who also operated a gristmill (County Road today dips to cross the stream that powered his mill, shortly before its intersection with Anderson Avenue). Several men who didn't flee or who resisted were taken prisoner; others were stabbed with bayonets, left for dead. One man, it was reported, brought to the ground by a bayonet, had his life spared only when a woman in his household physically placed herself between the raiders and the wounded man.

The County Road, then as now, swung to the west, crossed another stream (where an elementary school stands) and then swung north again at the Tenakill Brook (by the Demarest Railroad Station). The raiders continued along this roadway to where the Bogert and Tallman families had their farms. Both were among the more prominent families in Tappan and Closter. They owned many acres of farmland, and like most families of their standing in Closter, they were slave owners. Now eighty-nine years old and a great-grandfather several times over, Douwe Tallman had been among the first generation of Netherlanders to be born in the New World, his own father having been but three years old when his family sailed from Friesland for America. He was an elder at the Dutch church at Tappan. That Sunday afternoon he was run through with a bayonet. (Though it can't be confirmed, accounts written decades after would claim that he was trying to protect a strongbox of his important papers.)

He died two days later.

Douwe Tallman's son, Cornelius, who owned the property upon which the (Upper) Closter Dock stood, was among those taken prisoner into New York. Several of Cornelius's daughters, as well as a niece, were married to men who were killed or wounded that day, their houses and barns burned. (Cornelius himself would die two years later, in his sixties. It is tempting to speculate that his experience as a British prisoner hastened his death—tempting, but impossible to confirm.) Closter, though it sprawled across many miles, was in one sense a small place: most people knew one another well—including, of course, those who would eventually leave for British New York. Neighbors, though often living miles apart from one another, raised barns and built and maintained roads together, and they were often bound to one another through blood or marriage. It is not surprising that decades later, in the mid-nineteenth century, with many descendants of those who had stayed in Closter still living in the area, accounts of the raid would sometimes reappear in local newspapers and elsewhere. For the most part, it is simply impossible to verify the details of these later accounts, to sift family legend from fact. (Likewise, a refugee named Peter Myer was in fact killed during an action in Closter during March 1779, two months before the New Dock raid; it is impossible to verify whether his body was then desecrated. However, accounts favoring the Rebel side have usually portrayed Myer as little more than a horse thief.) The passions of the day continue to obscure the "facts on the ground"; what remains not obscured in the end is the passion itself, surprising and terrible, then as now.

Only two months later, in July, another raid was recorded in the *New Jersey Gazette*, this one from the Closter Dock:

> *Extract of a letter from New Barbadoes* [Hackensack], *July 22, 1779.*
>
> *On Sunday afternoon, the 10th inst. a party of refugees and tories, in number about 20, under the command of Lieut. Waller, (as it is said) landed at Closter-Dock, and advanced to the neighbourhood called Closter, from which they collected and drove off a considerable amount of cattle and horses, in order to carry them aboard a sloop, which they brought up for that purpose. They were pursued by Capt. Harring and Thomas Blanch, esq. At the head of a few of their neighbours, hastily collected, who recovered all the cattle except two and a calf, and all the horses save one and an old mare, which they had got aboard previous to the arrival of Capt. Harring.*
>
> *Capt. Harring took two prisoners, seven stand of arms and three suits of clothes, and obliged the enemy to cut their cable, conceal themselves below deck, and let their vessel drive with the tide, notwithstanding above 20 vessels in the river endeavored to protect them by cannonading Capt. Harring.*

A year later, in July 1780, General Wayne reconnoitered the two Closter Landings for General Washington, noting of the Lower Landing that "this road is at present Obstructed by felled trees & large rocks so that nothing but single footmen can pass & that with difficulty." The militia must have

Douwe Talema stone in Sauches Taves Begraven Ground, Demarest. *Courtesy of Ira Lieblich.*

decided to place obstructions on the road to help fend off the raiders—even at the cost of blocking their own farms' access to the river.

After the war, the New Dock, which had been owned by one of Closter's Loyalist families, came into the possession of the Huyler family (Captain John Huyler had been among the leaders of the militia). Through the nineteenth century this landing became known as Huyler's Landing, and it was reported that as many as forty wagons a day would bring farm goods there during harvest times. As farms gave way to suburbs, and then as the Palisades riverfront became parkland, this vital farm landing was all but forgotten. A brick house—called the Huyler Dock House by the Historic American Buildings Survey (HABS), probably built early in the nineteenth century and used as a boardinghouse for laborers—burned to the ground in the 1970s.

The Closter Dock, meanwhile, would become known as Alpine Landing. By the twentieth century, after the land there was acquired by the Palisades Interstate Park, a boat basin and a major ferry crossing to Yonkers would be established (the ferry closed in 1957, after the opening of the Tappan Zee Bridge upriver). A stone-and-timber house, probably dating to before the Revolution, still stands where the first docks were built; it is open to the public as a museum and called the Kearney House, for the family that lived in it through much of the nineteenth century. (Researching the early history of this house and the Closter Dock led me to Cornelius Tallman—and to Closter's bloody Revolutionary saga.) After the Interstate Park acquired the house in 1907 and renovated it, it was reported that "a cannon ball or two" had been dug out of its walls.

A few miles to the west, in Demarest, in my own lifetime wind and rain have made much of the writing on Douwe Tallman's gravestone all but unreadable. Fortunately, a second stone, with the text of the original reproduced, has been placed on the ground nearby.

Eric Nelsen

The writing on the stones ends with this sentence:

*To pay a Tribute of Respect to his
Memory and also to commemorate
the Manner of his Death, several of
his Relatives have erected this Stone.*

———•———

Eric Nelsen is a historical interpreter for the Palisades Interstate Park Commission and the director of the historic Kearney House at Alpine Boat Basin, where he keeps Nonesuch, *a twenty-three-foot sloop-rigged sailboat. He is the co-author of Arcadia's* Images of America: Palisades Interstate Park, *published in 2007.*

JOHN FELL

Patriot, POW, Diarist Extraordinaire

JIM WRIGHT

John Fell of Allendale is among the least-heralded of America's Founding Fathers—and no wonder. He is often remembered (if he is remembered at all) for participating in the Continental Congress and ratifying the U.S. Constitution.

In truth, Fell's greatest contributions came a bit earlier, when he led the Revolution in Bergen County and nearly died for those actions in a wretched British prison across the Hudson River, thirty miles from his Allendale home.

During those many months of captivity in the notorious Provost Jail in lower Manhattan, Fell kept a secret journal that documented for future generations Great Britain's deplorable treatment of American prisoners during the Revolution.

As Edwin Burrows, author of *Forgotten Patriots: The Untold Story of American Prisoners During the Revolutionary War*, explained in a newspaper interview in 2008: "John Fell's account is one of those little gems that laid hidden away in a box of papers at the Brooklyn Historical Society. He kept this diary in a tiny bound book, no bigger than a three-by-five note card. It really puts you in the moment when he talks about having no blankets in the winter and suffocating in the summer heat."

First, a bit of background: John Fell was born in New York City on February 5, 1721. According to *New Jersey Biographical and Genealogical Notes from the Volumes of the New Jersey Archives*, he "became the senior member of the firm of John Fell & Co., merchants in New York, at least as early as 1759, when they had several armed merchant vessels plying the seas. Eventually,

John Fell's House, Franklin Turnpike, Allendale. *Courtesy of Ira Lieblich.*

he purchased a tract of 220 acres…at or near Paramus [in what is now Allendale], in Bergen County. He called the place Petersfield."

Fell and his wife, Susanna, had a son, Peter R., born in 1752, and a daughter, Elizabeth, birth date unknown.

According to *Biographical and Genealogical Notes*, "From the beginning of the Revolution [John Fell] took a most positive stand in favor of his country, serving with great energy as Chairman of the Bergen County Committee [of Safety], in which capacity he gained the reputation of being 'a great Tory hunter.'

"He was a member of the Provincial Congress which met at Trenton in May, June and August, 1775, and of the Council in the first State Legislature, in 1776."

He became a common pleas judge in 1776 as well. Donald Whisenhunt, in his book on Fell's later Continental Congress journals, *Delegate from New Jersey*, adds that in June 1774, Fell "was the leader of a group of 328 citizens who signed patriotic resolutions at the Hackensack Courthouse pledging themselves to support and aid the resistance to Great Britain."

Fell's son, Peter, now in his twenties, soon joined the Patriot cause as well.

Being a thorn in the side of the British came at a price. After the British suffered defeats at the battles of Trenton and Princeton in late 1776 and early

1777, they retreated to New York City. On John Fell's home turf, sprawling Bergen County, Hessians loyal to the crown held posts in key locations until early spring and were constantly harassed by the New Jersey militia. Not surprisingly, the Loyalists retaliated. They raided several places in the county, seizing supplies and capturing opposition leaders. On April 22, 1777, a day after Peter R. Fell was named captain of the local Rebel force, Loyalists arrested John Fell at Petersfield in Allendale. Fell wrote in his journal the next day: "Last night I was taken prisoner from my house by 25 armed men who brought me down to Colonel Buskirk's at Bergen Point."

At that point, accounts differ. *Biographical and Genealogical Notes* tells the story this way—perhaps sweetened over time:

> *The two men* [Abraham Van Buskirk and John Fell] *had been well acquainted before the war, and when Fell was brought before Van Buskirk, the latter remarked: "Times have changed since we last met."*
>
> *"So I perceive," replied the prisoner.*
>
> *Van Buskirk, however, assured him that on account of their previous acquaintance he would give him a letter to General Robertson, in New York, with whom he was well acquainted, and this letter would doubtless insure him proper treatment. Fell was sent to New York and confined in the Provost Jail…*
>
> *General Robertson does not appear to have seen Fell until December 8th following, when he called upon him at the jail. Fell gave him the letter of Colonel Van Buskirk, which he read and then handed back, with a curious smile, to the prisoner, who found that the purport of the letter was that "John Fell was a great rebel and a notorious rascal."*

One of the nineteen prisoners who shared a cramped cell with John Fell was the celebrated Ethan Allen. In *A Narrative of Col. Ethan Allen's Captivity*, Allen recounted Fell's imprisonment, albeit with a bit of embroidery:

> *The stench of the gaol, which was very loathsome and unhealthy, occasioned a hoarseness of the lungs which proved fatal to many who were there confined, and reduced this gentleman* [John Fell] *near to the point of death; he was, indeed, given over by his friends who were about him, and he himself concluded he must die.*
>
> *I could not endure the thought that so worthy a friend to America should have his life stolen from him in such a mean, base and scandalous manner, and that his family and friends should be bereaved of so great and desirable a blessing as his further care, usefulness and example might prove to them.*

I therefore wrote a letter to General Robertson…There is so extraordinary a circumstance which intervened concerning this letter that it is worth noticing. Previous to sending it I exhibited the same to the gentleman on whose behalf it was written, for his approbation, and he forbid me to send it in the most positive and explicit terms; the reason he gave was that the enemy knew, by every morning's report, the condition of all the prisoners, his in particular he said, as he had been gradually coming to his end for a considerable time, and they very well knew it, and likewise determined it should be accomplished, as they had served many others; that to ask a favor would give the merciless enemy occasion to triumph over him in his last moments and therefore he would ask no favors from them, but had resigned himself to his fate.

Burrows, in his book *Forgotten Patriots*, says that Ethan Allen's letter on Fell's behalf to General Robertson "moved the hardhearted commandant to change his mind."

Early in January 1778, General Robertson released the gravely ill Fell to a nearby private home, where he slowly recovered.

When Fell left the Provost Jail, he took his secret journal with him—a journal that would have brought brutal punishment if his British captors had found it. Fell's journal remains significant to this day for the cruelties it documents.

As Danske Dandridge recounted in *American Prisoners of the Revolution*, published in the early 1900s and reprinted in 2006: "Mr. Fell's notes on his imprisonment present the best picture we can find of the condition of the Provost Jail during the term of his captivity."

Americans imprisoned there were jailed

without distinction of rank or character, amongst felons, a number of whom were under sentence of death: that their friends were not allowed to speak to them, even through the grates: that they were put on the scanty allowance of two pounds hard biscuit, and two pounds of raw pork per week, without fuel to dress it.

That they were frequently supplied with water from a pump where all kinds of filth was thrown, by which it was rendered obnoxious and unwholesome, the effects of which were to cause much sickness.

That good water could have been as easily obtained. That they were denied the benefit of a hospital; not permitted to send for medicine, nor to have the services of a doctor, even when in the greatest distress.

That married men and others who lay at the point of death were refused permission to have their wives or other relations admitted to see them. And that these poor women, for attempting to gain admittance, were often beaten from the prison door.

That commissioned officers, and others, persons of character and reputation, were frequently, without a cause, thrown into a loathsome dungeon, insulted in a gross manner, and vilely abused by a Provost Marshal, who was allowed to be one of the basest characters in the British army, and whose power was so unlimited, that he had caned an officer, on a trivial occasion; and frequently beaten the sick privates when unable to stand…

Neither pen, ink, or paper allowed [to prevent their treatment being made public], *the consequence of which indeed, the prisoners themselves dread, knowing the malignant disposition of their keeper.*

Here's a sampling of entries from Fell's secret prison journal:

May 31, 1777. Bad water; proposing buying tea-water, but refused. This night ten prisoners from opposite room ordered into ours, in all twenty.
June 10. Prisoners very sickly.
June 13. Melancholy scene, women refused speaking to their sick husbands, and treated cruelly by sentries.
June 26. Justice Moore died and was carried out.
July 12. Sergt. Keath took all pens and ink out of each room, and forbid the use of any on pain of the dungeon.
July 14. Jacobus Blauvelt died in the morning, buried at noon.
July 16. Capt. Ed. Travis brought into our room from the dungeon, where he had long been confined and cruelly treated.
Sept. 4. Horrid scenes of whipping.
Nov. 16. Jail exceedingly disagreeable—many miserable and shocking objects, nearly starved with cold and hunger—miserable prospect before me.
Nov. 24. Six tailors brought here from prison ship to work in making clothes for prisoners. They say the people on board are very sickly. Three hundred sent on board reduced to one hundred.
Dec. 10. Prisoners very sickly and die very fast from the hospitals and prison ships.

As Fell recounted in those November 24 and December 10 entries, conditions on the British prison ships in New York Harbor during that period were even more horrendous than in the Provost Jail.

Here is a sad and little-known footnote to this essay: far more Americans died on those prison ships and other New York City prisons than on the battlefield in the Revolution.

In his preface to *Forgotten Patriots*, Edwin Burrows writes that the number of captives there may actually have "exceeded 30,000 and that 18,000 (60 percent) or more of them did not survive—well over *twice* the number of American soldiers and seamen who fell in battle, now believed to have been around 6,800. It is a mean, ugly story. It is also a story that enlarges our understanding of how the United States was made—not merely by bewigged gentlemen who thought deeply, talked well, and wrote gracefully, but thousands upon thousands of mostly ordinary people who believed in something they considered worth dying for."

Just how horrendous those conditions were would not be as well-documented today if John Fell of Allendale had not spent nearly a year in the cause of liberty as a British prisoner of war.

POSTSCRIPT

In 1778, the year Fell was released from the Provost Jail, the New Jersey Legislature elected him to be one of its two delegates to the Continental Congress. He served two years.

According to *Biographical and Genealogical Notes*, John Fell "was evidently a man of considerable means and accustomed to live in good style, and was frequently the guest of John Adams and other distinguished leaders."

For a full year, Fell kept a detailed journal that documented the day-to-day activities of the Founding Fathers.

As Donald Whisenhunt writes in his introduction to *Delegate from New Jersey*, "Fell's diary and the Journals of the Continental Congress… show him to be a man of firm fiscal responsibility. He was reluctant to support movements to inflate the already weak currency and to increase the nation's indebtedness, which was already so great that some questioned the government's solvency. Despite this concern, he nevertheless voted to do what he considered necessary for a vigorous prosecution of the war."

Jim Wright

JOHN FELL: ONCE A PATRIOT, ALWAYS A...

According to *Biographical and Genealogical Notes*, John Fell sold his Allendale estate, known as Petersfield, on November 1, 1793, to John H. Thompson, a merchant of New York City, for £2,000. "He then removed to New York, Dutchess County, taking up his residence with his son, Peter, and died [on May 15, 1798] at Coldenham."

According to that same reference book, Fell's son Peter "devoted himself so zealously to the service [of his country] and exposed himself so recklessly that he became hopelessly crippled with rheumatism...He died at Coldenham, Oct. 6, 1789, age 37."

Jim Wright is a longtime journalist and author with an interest in Bergen County history and natural history. Wright became fascinated by the life and sometimes trying times of John Fell after Wright moved to Allendale and discovered that the stately house across the Franklin Turnpike once belonged to a member of the Continental Congress. He has had seven books published, including three coffee-table books on Allendale, Central America and Hawk Mountain in Pennsylvania—all of which have substantial history sections. He was an award-winning staff writer for the Bergen Record *for more than three decades and has written about everything from a historic 1848 Paterson fire to efforts to save the Steuben House.*

Hessian Accounts of the Expedition to Hopperstown in April 1780

Annotated by Lieutenant Colonel Donald M. Londahl-Smidt, USAF-Ret

Although several articles concerning the expedition to Hopperstown (now Ho-Ho-Kus), New Jersey, in April 1780 have been published, none includes Hessian accounts. This seems odd since Hessians made up the principal part of the force, a Hessian officer was in overall command and a German officer commanded the cavalry detachment. To correct this oversight, we present translations of the German accounts of the expedition. The original manuscripts are in the Hessisches Staatsarchiv Marburg. Transcripts and translations of all of them, except the letter of Captain von Diemar, are in the Lidgerwood Collection of Hessian Transcripts at Morristown National Historical Park.

Report from Major Du Buy to His Excellency Lieutenant General von Knyphausen

At the beginning of the War of the American Revolution, Johann Christian Du Buy was the senior captain in the Hessen-Cassel Fusilier Regiment von Dittfurth. On February 11, 1776, shortly before beginning his march and voyage to America, Du Buy was promoted to major in the Regiment von Trümbach (renamed von Bose in January 1779). He was also appointed brigade major to the Hessian corps, which position he resigned in July 1779. As a reward for his leadership during the expedition to Hopperstown and other actions in which he was involved, Landgrave Friedrich II awarded Du Buy the Hessian order *Pour la Vertu Militaire*. In November 1780 Du Buy was promoted to lieutenant colonel and two months later was appointed quartermaster general to the Hessian corps in America.

Under Du Buy's command, the Regiment von Bose went south to Virginia with Major General Alexander Leslie in October 1780 and then continued to South Carolina. As part of Lord Cornwallis's army, Du Buy and his regiment participated with distinction in the Battle of Guilford Courthouse, North Carolina, on March 15, 1781, and then accompanied Cornwallis to Virginia. Fortunately for Du Buy, he was ordered to come to New York to take up his duties as quartermaster general of the Hessian forces in America and escaped being captured at Yorktown. In November 1783, he left New York as part of the British evacuation, wintered in England and finally returned home to Hessen-Cassel in the spring of 1784.

D.D. Greenwich [New York], the 17ᵀᴴ April, 1780

According to your Excellency's gracious command I embarked on the evening of the 15ᵗʰ. instant after 8 o'clock with 230 [sic: 250] men of the von Mirbach and von Bose Regiments, 12 Jägers and 50 men of Colonel Robinson's Provincial [Loyal American] Regiment below Fort Knyphausen, and landed at 9 o'clock at Fort Lee on the coast of New Jersey. I reached English Neighborhood with the detachment after 10 o'clock, where I halted in order to wait for the detachment of cavalry, consisting of 120 men, which had been transported from Staten Island to Bergen Neck. The same joined me at midnight, and we at once continued our march to Newbridge, which we reached at about 3 o'clock on the morning of the 16ᵗʰ, and met there, contrary to all expectations, a picket of Continental troops consisting of one officer and twenty-four men, who had been sent from Paramus the evening before in order to waylay a number of Rebel deserters, and bring them back. The sentry on the bridge fired but the picket had no time to defend the bridge but had to save themselves by running away in the dark. The officer and three men were taken prisoners. I left Captain [David] Reichhold of the Mirbach Regiment there with 50 men in order to ensure our return to Newbridge. At daybreak the detachment arrived at Paramus, when I learned to my great annoyance that a body of Rebels, which had been stationed at that place, was no longer there but was quartered at Hopperstown, 1½ miles further. Although there was no question of taking them by surprise under these circumstances, I did not like to give up the plan all together, as I hoped the cavalry would come upon the enemy suddenly, and be able to attack them before they could retire to the mountains. Consequently I advanced to Paramus Bridge with the utmost speed; the Rebel picket posted on the bridge took to flight, but was overtaken and partly captured, partly hewn down. Hereupon the cavalry attacked Hopperstown and the infantry followed as rapidly as it could; the Rebels had no time to form ranks although they could see us marching across the plain between Paramus and Hopperstown but had to retire as best as they could. Some of them threw themselves into a stone house, the quarters of Major [Thomas L.] *Byles, who was the officer in command of them, and defended it obstinately. Captain* [Friedrich] *von Diemar attacked the same, assisted by the Dragoons and Hussars who were the first to come up, with great courage and success. Many of the fugitives were captured or killed. After causing the aforesaid house to be set on fire, and as there did not seem to be any likelihood of doing more harm to the scattered enemy, I gave the order to march back. Hardly had we crossed Sadler* [Saddle] *Creek near Paramus when Rebels, mostly militia, appeared and began to harass the rear guard. Their number increased every moment and they annoyed both flanks and rear guard so much, that we could only continue our march under a constant fire, which lasted until we came near Fort Lee, where I took my stand with half the detachment, while I caused the other half to be ferried across together with the wounded and prisoners, there not being sufficient flat-bottomed boats to take us all at once. When the boats returned, I embarked as speedily as possible with the rest, but we were pursued so closely that we were shot at even in the boats and were obliged to leave a wounded man behind. Major Byles, who had commanded the Rebels at Hopperstown, as well as those in the house, was captured together with 6 officers and 54 privates, but he was left behind on parole owing to severe wounds. As far as I can judge, about 40 Rebels remained on the field during the attack on Hopperstown and the march back. Your Excellency will see particulars on the loss on our side from the lists that have arrived; this is greater than I had imagined, but still it is no wonder when I consider that we were under constant fire from 6 o'clock in the morning till 5 in the evening. The wounds are mostly slight and it is especially gratifying to me to know that I did not leave any wounded or exhausted men behind except the one, but that we brought all the others with us. I cannot refrain from mentioning that all the officers and privates of the detachment, cavalry as well as infantry, behaved in a most exemplary manner and exhibited true bravery and fortitude during this arduous expedition. And should not give Lieutenant* [Carl Levin]

Marquard his due if I forgot to mention to your Excellency that he was of much assistance to me and contributed much to the success of the expedition by his zeal.

F.C. du BUY

JOURNAL OF THE REGIMENT VON BOSE

On the 14th April 1780 a detachment of cavalry from Staten Island consisting of 120 men of the Seventeenth Dragoon Regiment, the Queen's Rangers, Diemar's Hussars and Lieutenant Col. [sic: Lieutenant] *Stuart's Volunteers, and one of infantry, 312 men strong, from York Island consisting of 12 Jägers, 150 men of the von Bose Regiment, 100 men of the von Mirbach Regiment and 50 men of the Loyal Americans, under command of Maj. du Buy, landed in Jersey. The cavalry crossed from Staten Island to Bergen Neck and the infantry were ferried over the North River at Fort Lee in the evening in order to join each other in the English Neighborhood; the whole then marched to Newbridge and Hackensack, which place they reached between two and three o'clock on the morning of the 16th. At this place they attacked a patrol of the Rebels, the officer of which was taken prisoner with three men; the rest, however, took to flight. Maj. du Buy continued his march to Paramus, reached the church at daybreak and there discovered that the Rebels had retreated to Hopperstown. This march was continued and on the bridge at Saddle Creek a picket was found to be posted, who fired, but the men were shot dead and taken prisoners by the advance guard of the cavalry. The cavalry was ordered to advance, reached Hopperstown very swiftly and with the greatest courage began to attack a strong body of infantry in a connected cantonment. In the meanwhile the infantry had marched up and the Rebels fled. Several houses in which they were hiding were surrounded and they were taken prisoners. On the return march several parties of militia, which may have been posted elsewhere previously, pursued this corps, moved slowly round the detachment during the march and fired continuously upon them from different directions, inflicting considerable injury upon the detachment. The detachment fired uninterruptedly and several soldiers had soon exhausted all their cartridges. The firing on both sides continued during the retreat as far as Fort Lee where, at the foot of the hill, the boats were moored ready for embarkation. The cavalry took the same road back to Staten Island by which they had come. Between three and four o'clock in the afternoon the detachment of infantry descended the hill and lost on the road and while embarking in the boats several men killed and wounded or captured. When all were across each detachment rejoined its regiment.*

List of Killed, Wounded and Missing: -

Seventeenth Dragoons and 1 horse killed [sic]*; 1 horse and 3 men wounded.*
Queen's Rangers Hussars: 3 men and three horses killed; 1 man and 2 horses wounded.
Diemar's Hussars: 2 men and 1 horse wounded.
Staten Island Volunteers: 3 privates wounded.
Hessian Jägers: 1 man wounded.
Mirbach: 1 killed and 11 wounded.
v. Bose: 2 killed and 5 wounded.
TOTAL: 7 men and 4 horses killed, 2 non-commissioned officers, 29 men and 4 horses wounded.
Two wounded men, one of them belonging to the v. Bose Regiment, were taken prisoners owing to their wounds.

List of the Rebels' Loss.

40 killed, 53 taken prisoners, 51 wounded.
The Major in command and 1 officer had to be left owing to their severe wounds, otherwise 6 officers were brought in as prisoners.

ORDER BOOK OF THE REGIMENT VON MIRBACH

[April] the 15th. A captain, two subalterns, nine non-commissioned officers, and 100 privates, all chosen men, of the Regiment von Mirbach, are to assemble in the street at Commissary Steward's quarters this evening at sundown, or about six-thirty, and await Maj. DuBuy's orders. The men are to take nothing with them but cooked rations for one day, and rum. They are to wear their old uniforms, but not carry blankets. Therefore only healthy and robust men are to be chosen so that they will not fall into the enemy's hands due to fatigue.

The 18th—Order, Headquarters, New York

His Excellency Lieutenant General von Knyphausen desires that his satisfaction be expressed in public orders to Major DuBuy of the Hessian Regiment von Bose for his good conduct during the attack and assault against a host of rebels, who were cantoned on the morning of the sixteenth of this month, at Hopperstown in New Jersey, and to the officers and soldiers under his command, for their good behavior at that time. His Excellency is obligated to Captain von Diemar and the troop of cavalry under his command, for their determined attack against some houses at that place, which were occupied by rebels. The General also thanks Lieutenant Cran[s]ton of the Navy, and the officers and sailors under his command, for the good service rendered with their flatboats.

JOURNAL OF THE REGIMENT VON MIRBACH

16 April 1780—everything remained quiet. During the night of 16–17 April, Major Du Buy and 250 men who were taken from the von Mirbach and von Bose Regiments, were joined by Robinson's Corps, and ordered on an expedition into Jersey. As soon as the detachment reached the vicinity of Fort Lee, without having encountered the least resistance, the troops were allowed to rest pending the arrival of Captain von Diemar with his Hussars and some cavalry, which were set across the North River near Paulus Hook. Toward noon the latter arrived at the mentioned fort, and both commands continued their march to Woodbridge [sic: New Bridge] *where an enemy picket was posted.*

To cover the left flank Captain Reichhold and fifty men had to occupy the bridge and the major went with the rest of the troops to Hoppertown, where several hundred rebels were stationed. These were driven into flight without our side losing a man. During this affair, a major, five officers and 87 men were captured. After the expedition was ended, the major and his prisoners returned. As soon as the Rebels were aware that several skirmishes had taken place to their disadvantage between our troops and theirs, all the troops in the area were assembled together, and Captain Reichhold, who commanded the rear, had one of his men killed and eleven wounded.

Journal of the Feldjäger Corps

Apr. 16—A detachment of 250 men, and one non commissioned officer and 15 Jägers under Major DuBuy made an incursion into Jersey, where the enemy had assembled, attacked them, and captured six officers and 51 men, and killed another twenty men, without suffering any losses. On the return march, our force was harassed all the way to the boats by the militia, and men who had run from the action. This resulted in two killed and seventeen wounded. Among the wounded was the Jäger non commissioned officer.

Captain Friedrich Baron von Diemar to the Hereditary Prince Wilhelm of Hessen-Cassel, Reigning Count of Hesse-Hanau

At the beginning of 1776, Friedrich Baron von Diemar was a lieutenant in the Hanoverian Infantry Regiment von Goldacher serving as a German aide-de-camp to Lieutenant General James Murray, governor of Minorca, where Diemar's regiment was stationed. In 1778 he entered British service as a titular lieutenant in the Third Battalion of the Sixtieth (or Royal American) Regiment of Foot. In April 1779, Diemar was appointed commander of a troop of Hussars composed mainly but not exclusively of the Brunswick and Hessen-Hanau soldiers who had been captured during Burgoyne's campaign in 1777 and had escaped to New York City from American captivity. The former POWs returned to their respective services on May 15, 1780, and the remainder were transferred to the Queen's Rangers in April 1781. Diemar remained in America until April 1783, when he departed New York for six months' leave in Europe. He was placed on half-pay when the Third and Fourth Battalions of the Sixtieth Regiment were disbanded at the end of the war.

Outpost at Mile Square on New York Island, July 18, 1780

I can honestly praise your Highness' troops' bravery and devotion to duty. On 16 April in the affair at Hopperstown in New Jersey where I with 112 men cavalry attacked 250 Rebels of the 3rd Pennsylvania Inf Regt who were posted in houses and in the fields. I made them yield with the loss of 39 dead and wounded and took a major, 2 captains, 4 subalterns and 52 [men] prisoner.

The Hessian Major Dupuy commanded the infantry, which covered the withdrawal of the cavalry through a large woods, but not favorably, because of a fatiqueing march of 27 English miles to get here, as they "en debandade" withdrew to a rocky mountain near Hopperstown. General Knyphausen issued complimentary thanks in his orders to all my men except Sgt Johannes Moerschel [see below].

The above-mentioned Sgt of the noble Artillery, who was employed as quartermaster in the squadron, returned my goodness with deceit. After fraud and horse tradding with loyal residents, he secretly left his post and received from me 4 months' general arrest with the provost.

Head Quarters New York 18th. April 1780.

His Excellency Lieutenant General Knyphausen desires his thanks may be given in publick orders, to Major Dupuy of the Hessian Regt. de Bose, for his good conduct in attacking and forcing a body of Rebels cantooned in Hopperstown in Jersey, upon the morning of the 16th. Inst: and to the Officers and Soldiers under his command for their behaviour upon that occasion.

His Excellency is very much obliged to Captain Diemar and the body of Cavalry under his command, for the determin'd attack upon the different houses possessed by the Rebels at that place, and the Gen. is indebted to Lieutenant Cranston of the Navy and to the Officers and Seamen under his Orders for their services with the flat boats.

Donald M. Londahl-Smidt is a retired Air Force and commercial bank officer. He holds an MA in history from the University of Delaware. A Fellow of the Company of Military Historians, he has been awarded that organization's Distinguished Service Award. Lieutenant Colonel Londahl-Smidt is a member of the board of directors and editorial committee and the director of military research for the Johannes Schwalm Historical Association, a society dedicated to researching the history of the Hessian and other German troops that fought on the British side during the Revolutionary War. He has co-authored one book, written numerous published articles and given many lectures to various audiences on Revolutionary War history.

Robert Erskine

Minemaster and Mapmaker for the American Revolution

William Neumann

It is quite probable that you are unfamiliar with the life of Robert Erskine. Described by his most ardent biographer, Albert Heusser, as "The Forgotten General," there may be volumes unwritten about this little-acclaimed Patriot who served America with high distinction. This Scottish entrepreneur arrived on the cusp of the Revolution to find his true fortune in living in the most interesting of times and associating closely with leaders who would change the world. The humble manager of an iron mining company became a confidant of George Washington and rose to become the most prolific mapmaker of the war, producing more than 250 maps for the Patriot cause in just over two years.

Robert Erskine was born on September 7, 1735, sixteen miles from Edinburgh, Scotland, in the village of Dunfermline. The village was of some renown as the local Presbyterian abbey holds the remains of seven kings and two queens, as well as the grave of its beloved Reverend Ralph Erskine. From his two marriages Reverend Erskine fathered a total of fourteen children, with Robert the only surviving sibling from his second union, with Margaret Simson. Robert was educated in the local Dunfermline school but had the opportunity to enter the University of Edinburgh as early as 1748. By 1752 he was fully enrolled and became sufficiently educated to anticipate a future position at the University of Glasgow. He did not fill that post but took up a business partnership with a Mr. Swinton in 1759. This proved to be a terrible failure, and worse: Swinton left Erskine in complete debt to their creditors when he sailed to the Americas, never to be heard from again. In 1762 Erskine was "detained" for the partnership's debts but shortly released to work out repayments.

A Robert Erskine drawing of his 1765 Platometer. *Courtesy of the New Jersey Historical Society, William Neumann Photography.*

This hardship seemed to propel Robert Erskine in an entrepreneurial direction, and he began an intense period of engineering inventiveness. He evolved a previous plan for a hydraulic pump and had it produced for use. By 1765 he was lodging in London and his constant stream pump was catching the interest of the scientific community. His divergent interests and abilities were also evident in his "Platometer," an instrument to "find the Latitude and variation of the Needle at Sea; at any time of the day, by two observations of the Sun." His ability as a draughtsman was admired as well, and for a time he held the position of land surveyor and engineer. Erskine studied and suggested improvements to London's waterways and added his voice to those trying to eliminate the scourge of smallpox. During this joyous time, he married Elizabeth. Sadly, their only progeny, daughter Sarah, would not live to maturity.

As Robert Erskine rose through the trials of small business debtor to notable inventor and London socialite, a commercial venture took shape on the northeast coast of the American colonies that would soon dictate his entire future.

In 1720 a profitable copper deposit had been discovered by a branch of the Schuyler family in the colony of New Jersey, between the Hackensack and Passaic Rivers and close to Second River (now Belleville). Somewhat successful mining operations had also commenced in 1740 around the northern Bergen County area of Ringwood (now in Passaic County). As a result, a mining and export partnership created in 1763 by German merchant Peter Hasenclever and backed by a London syndicate began searching for additional New Jersey sites to extract and refine ore from the colony.

Hasenclever fortunately read a March 5, 1764 *New York Mercury* advertisement for "a new well built furnace; good iron mines near the same; two forges…situated on a good stream 28 miles from Acquacknanung Landing and 36 miles from Newark." For £5,000 Hasenclever took possession of the Ringwood Company and quickly added other available land parcels at Ringwood, Long Pond and Charlotteburg. The combined fifteen thousand acres became the home of the substantial American Iron Company. In a little over two years' time, the company had a vast array of mines, four furnaces and seven forges, employing nearly three hundred people and shipping its fine grade iron to England. It also harvested furs, timber, hemp and potash and shipped those off to the mother country as was required by the one-sided trade restrictions imposed on the American colonies.

"Baron" Hasenclever created dwellings, farms, stores, mills, roads, races and dams to and from his operations as he oversaw a growing population of workers and their families. Iron-making technology was imported from Germany and helped to form the future of the United States iron industry. Hasenclever sought to acquire vast amounts of land in Bergen County, the colony of New York and even into Nova Scotia; however, by 1769 his credit had run out and his syndicate recalled him to London, where he was declared bankrupt.

In the winter of 1769–70, American Iron was threatened by total collapse and ruin. In its attempt to resurrect its company, the London syndicate reached out to an unlikely savior. The syndicate made Erskine an offer, and it took him quite a few months to decide to become an onsite manager of the American Iron Company in the wilderness areas of the northern New Jersey and southern New York colonies. It is not clear how the company found Robert Erskine. His prominence in London was rising but he had little managerial and no mining experience.

During the remainder of the year, Erskine threw himself into preparation for his new profession by visiting and consulting intensively with Great Britain's leading mining and forging operations. He obtained mining samples, observed smelting and casting productions and made detailed notes on the architecture and creation of the empire's best forges.

His preparations propelled him resolutely toward America. Then, during the waning days of 1769, there was a renewed interest in his constant stream pump. He was invited to present it before the membership of the Royal Society of London. With the sponsorship of incoming society President Sir John Pringle and the much admired Benjamin Franklin, Erskine was elected as a Fellow of the Royal Society on January 31, 1771. Through the remainder of his life his signature was followed by "F.R.S." (Fellow of the Royal Society) and it appears in his gravestone inscription. This momentous acclamation must have been a serious paradox as it afforded him substantial opportunities in Great Britain but carried far less currency in the colonies. However, it acquainted him with Dr. Benjamin Franklin, another society Fellow, and Franklin's advocacy for the American colonies' independence.

Robert Erskine did not look back and set his mind toward his appointment to the management of the American Iron Company's mines and forges. The company instructed him as to his limitations and obligations and he knew he would first co-manage with the then current caretaker, John Jacob Faesch. His salary was set at £370 per annum plus a 5 percent share of the net profits. He and Mrs. Erskine set sail for America in April 1771 and, after a voyage of two months, landed June 5 in the port of New York City.

London notice of Robert Erskine's 1764 constant stream pump. *Courtesy of the New Jersey Historical Society, William Neumann Photography.*

Erskine arrived in Ringwood, New Jersey, and settled in with provisions and directions from his colonial representatives in New York City. It is apparent that his first year was a tough apprenticeship, but he was soon busy improving roads and utilizing his engineering skills to improve the efficiency of the mining operations. Unfortunately, the American Iron Company was hard to deal with regarding funding and allotting for needed expenses. A plan to raise cash by selling off surplus land yielded no takers. Erskine was forced to set up derivative funding by trading raw iron bars at market houses for credit and to barter to maintain the cash flow needed for raw materials and production. During this time he was able to open the Bellegrove Store, a few miles south of Suffern's Tavern in the Ramapo area, first as a company supply depot and eventually as a well-known trading post for the region. He found that by trading essentials for wages and local services his overhead was substantially reduced.

The Erskines assimilated into the local social set that included the neighboring families of Sloat, Board, Noble, Townsend and Ward. Many of the regional iron competitors of the American Iron Company became Erskine friends, such as the Brinkerhoffs, the Jacksons of Rockaway, the Fords of Morristown and the Erskines' neighbor, Lord Stirling (William Alexander). All were deeply affected by the colonial restrictions put on American business by Great Britain. Lord Stirling was appointed surveyor-general of New Jersey in 1756. He was an outspoken Patriot who would rise to the rank of major general and be captured in the Battle of Long Island. Discussion of the mounting division between the colonies and England was certainly a topic of enormous concern. As Britain struggled to finance its unending string of wars, it stepped up the taxation and financial exploitation of colonial America. The Erskines were present in America when the Boston Massacre demonstrated the extent to which British oppression was headed. Could this have been a first true sign for Erskine as to how his loyalty would be tested?

The Regulatory Acts of 1774 were a further hindrance to Erskine. In an October letter to his employers, he expressed his concern that a serious conflict was inevitable and stated that "the (British) rulers at home have gone too far." He worried that during a rebellion the operations he had so carefully rescued could be destroyed through chaos and lawlessness.

As the Battles of Lexington and Concord played out in April 1775, Robert Erskine must have fully realized the potential danger to his family, his livelihood and his new homeland. Perhaps as an act of self-preservation, he quickly organized one of the first New Jersey militias from amongst his workmen. It was a smart move as it forestalled the loss of these workers to other militias, set up a police force to secure his operations and gave credence to his growing patriotism. In May 1775, Erskine firmly stated to his London syndicate that it should be "explicit in declaring the situation of this country, which is beyond dispute indissolubly united against the British Ministry and their acts, to which the Americans will never subscribe but in characters of blood." The British occupation of New York steeled Erskine's patriotic resolve and his strategic importance. Ringwood, situated on the far side of the "neutral ground" between the British army in New York City and the Continental troops in the Highlands, was now perceived as a key outpost and a potential stronghold of security, and Robert Erskine was its master. In August, Erskine was commissioned captain of his formed militia. During the entirety of the war, marauders made many attempts to penetrate his defenses but only succeeded when Erskine was absent.

But Robert Erskine was not a sunshine Patriot ensconced behind an iron wall. Extant letters to General John Morin Scott of the New York Militia detail his 1776 plan to create and install a Marine "chevaux-de-frise" across the Hudson River to scuttle British ships headed offensively upriver. These heavily chained sharp wood and iron obstructions would prevent warships from flanking the American army remaining at the top of Manhattan and attacking the Continentals' outposts up the Hudson. In a letter to General Scott,

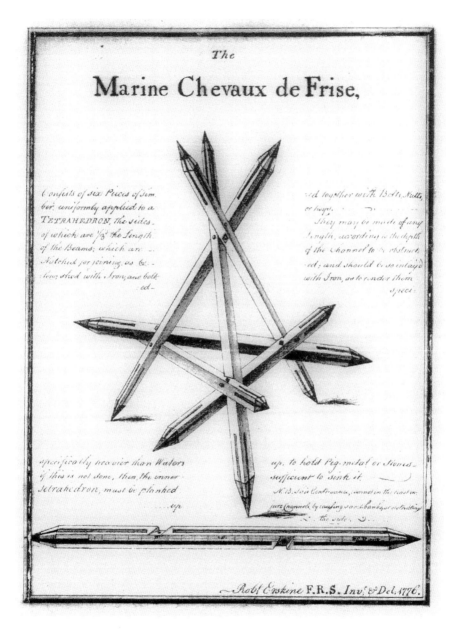

A Robert Erskine–illustrated explanation of his Marine chevaux-de-frise, or tetrahedron. *Courtesy of Ringwood Manor, Ringwood State Park, William Neumann Photography.*

Erskine stated, "I shall be happy if this invention could be put in practice soon enough to incommode our enemies at New York." Unfortunately his methods were not immediately adopted, and another chevaux-de-frise design was hastily installed and proved to be ineffective. During the war much of the massive chain links and iron spikes needed for these river defenses, as well as cannonballs, musket shot and cooking stoves, were manufactured in Erskine forges.

Ringwood was a stopping point on the highly strategic road from Philadelphia, through Trenton and Morristown and north to West Point. As the British cut off communication along the eastern seaboard, this inland road became extremely important. Robert Erskine was determined to keep his forges and mines working, and he traveled extensively to drum up new business throughout New Jersey and the adjoining colonies of Pennsylvania and New York.

As Robert Erskine journeyed, he produced his own maps. At one point he provided maps of the Ringwood area to General Charles Lee. The creation of this first map was aided by his fellow Patriot, William Alexander, Lord Stirling. Erskine had already mapped the New Windsor, New York area where a future chevaux-de-frise would be placed. This experience proved to be providential.

General George Washington traveled frequently between Morristown and the Hudson River Valley and had occasion to pass through Ringwood several times. At a personal meeting in Pompton, Erskine displayed some of his maps to Washington. An experienced surveyor, the general recognized the craftsmanship and detail of Erskine's work. Washington also realized how dependent his recent victories had been on knowledge of terrain and geography. George Washington believed that Erskine was a committed and trustworthy Patriot and a man of outstanding reliability. So it was that on July 17, 1777, General Washington recommended to the Committee of the Continental Congress that Robert Erskine become geographer and surveyor-general to the American army.

It took Erskine a half-year to cede some control of the mining operations in order to devote more of his time to mapping for the Continental army. He started traveling more between West Point and Philadelphia, sometimes with the army and sometimes only with his assistants, who included Lieutenant Benjamin Lodge, Captain John Watkins and Simeon DeWitt, his appointed understudy. DeWitt would eventually assume much of Erskine's duty after 1780.

Many of Robert Erskine's maps consisted of rough field sketches accurate as to terrain and geographic features but on a large scale of a mile to an inch. They were made by traversing the area recording measurements and bearings and then reconciled on a "Plain–Table." These were refined into smaller-scale extractions plotted on a conic grid in which the prime meridian was New York City. Many surveys and maps were produced on the personal order of Washington in anticipation of his strategic needs. Washington carried his own personal pocket versions of Erskine's maps throughout the war.

In the first six months of Erskine's employment as mapmaker he turned out 91 maps, and in 1779, approximately 160 more. In all, Erskine and his crew of upward a dozen men produced approximately 250 maps that covered areas of Connecticut, Pennsylvania and New York. By far the most maps were produced in New Jersey, with many local to northern Bergen County. Many of Erskine's maps are invaluable today as some of the first renderings of Bergen and Passaic Counties. Excellent collections of his work reside in the New Jersey and New York Historical Societies and the New York Public Library. Some of these maps have numerous comments inscribed by Washington's hand.

In 1779 Washington requested that General Erskine join the army at Morristown, possibly to protect his valuable supply of maps and the mapmaker himself. During much of this time Erskine attended Masonic

Composite photograph of the Robert Erskine grave site and inscription on his grave cover at Ringwood State Park. *Courtesy William Neumann Photography.*

convocations along with Washington. Erskine was also entreated to join the Army of the South, as much of the military action was focusing on Tory strongholds in the southern colonies. It seems that he did not commit to that idea and begged out to attend to his wife, home and business in New Jersey.

The Ringwood Manor that Robert Erskine called home would comfort him in his final days of early autumn 1780. Erskine was surveying the Hudson Highlands around September 18 for his Map #113—"Roads between Sufferns, Tappan, Kakiate, Paramus, Dobbs Ferry, Clarkstown"— when, it is believed, he caught cold from overexposure. He spent some of his last days working on this and two other map extractions that are now held in the New York Historical Society. Robert Erskine was overcome with fever and died at Ringwood on October 2, 1780, at the age of forty-five. It was just nine years and four months since he had first stepped onto his new homeland.

To date there have been no portraits discovered of this important but relatively unknown Patriot. Robert Erskine, F.R.S., is buried in Ringwood Manor's old cemetery along with early ironworkers and Revolutionary War soldiers. His enduring maps and his simple grave site are final reminders of how a common man gave his full measure in guiding a new nation to liberty and freedom.

———•———

William Neumann is a professional photographer, local historian and preservationist, and the author of Rutherford: A Brief History *(The History Press 2008). He is a past chairman of the Rutherford Historic Preservation Commission and current member of the Bergen County Historic Preservation Advisory Board.*

THE REVOLUTION AMONG US:
Terror and Tragedy in the Neutral Ground

NANCY TERHUNE

T his is a story about the Revolution that we do not teach our young children.

The untaught story of the War for Independence in Bergen County is one that none of us with Bergen roots wants to claim as our own, much less make a memorable lesson to the next generation.

It's difficult enough to explain the oxymoronic Retreat to Victory and why this *particular* retreat was not a shameful failure but a world-class success. Even children may be suspicious that the epic tale of a victorious retreat may be revisionist history, the spackling-over of something terribly botched.

Tell them that it isn't. And if you don't know the story of the Retreat to Victory, learn it and tell your children that what happened here may have saved the cause of independence.

As for the untaught story—you decide.

It may be enough to say that there were many heroes here, hundreds of them, and nearly all never wore the uniform of an army.

> *Let them who are in the midst of it depart out...for there shall be great distress in the land, and wrath upon this people...And they shall fall by the edge of the sword, and shall be led away captive.*
>
> *Luke 21:22–24*

The War for Independence was not supposed to come here. Bergen County was not to be a battleground. The war, on any count, was anticipated by both sides to be a short one. "A single successful battle next year will settle the whole," wrote Thomas Paine in December 1776.

Sandwiched between the British—who occupied the whole of the city of New York and Long Island with thousands of Loyalist troops and mercenaries, vast weaponry and a fleet—and a significant portion of the Continental army camped permanently in the Hudson Highlands, the area encompassing Bergen County and southeastern Orange County (now Rockland), New York, was an implicit neutral ground. Neither side wanted to engage in proximity to one of its strongholds.

Although the British placed troops in the southernmost corner of Bergen County, the spy-and-supply garrison should have made for no more than tense standoffs and policing actions. Residents of the neutral ground should have found themselves in a reasonably safe buffer zone, waiting for news of battles in distant places; some of its sons gone to fight elsewhere while their families maintained at least a semblance of prewar status quo.

There were no grand battles here, and certainly no pivotal ones from which tales of glory might be derived. So how can the fact that this was one of the most treacherous and terrifying places in the colonies for over a half-decade be explained?

What happened in the wartime neutral ground is one of the darkest and most prolonged sorrows of the war: the great toll of the Revolutionary War here was on its civilian inhabitants.

In a swath through the narrow Hackensack and Saddle River Valleys, from Bergen Point to Tappan, and for nearly the entirety of the war, those who remained and who professed or were suspected of Whiggish allegiance were under constant threat of being ambushed, assaulted, robbed or removed to prisons of unspeakable horror. Their homes, fields and businesses were looted, burned or both, often by their neutral ground neighbors in or out of uniform. Some were violated multiple times. Countless were wounded. Some were murdered. Women were abused and injured. Wives were left beyond their abilities to cope, with sole responsibility—temporary or permanent—for farms, businesses and livelihoods, or became impoverished widows. Foraging raids by British and Tory troops and, finally, the Continentals themselves left only what food and livestock had not been hidden. When controlled forages by Continental troops devolved into "anything goes," the Patriot citizenry didn't know whether to pray any longer for the protection of the army or wish to be abandoned to whatever fate might find them.

Though not constant, the attacks against citizens were a consistent pulse throughout the war, keeping the residents of the neutral ground in perpetual fear. They left their beds to spend nights in the woods. They were terrified to be in their fields alone. Many Patriots gave up altogether. Their neighbors witnessed them trailing after the enemy's troops, newly minted Tories on their way to refugee lives.

Unfortunately the media of the day regularly amplified the fear level to a frenzy, often printing grossly inflated accounts.

Shifting, unknown or duplicitous loyalties kept relations between neighbors—even family members—taut with suspicion and the entire population vigilant. Neighbor against neighbor, cousin against cousin, occasionally brother against brother: these were facts of everyday life. And to the shocking actions of the largely homegrown Tory troops was added the threat of violent crimes by gangs of lawless marauders.

Betrayed by their own, abandoned by the Continental army, terrified, bereft and broken, the people of the neutral ground were refugees on their own lands. Unlike most of the colonies, with their transient battles and skirmishes, danger and evil came to reside here, dug in for the duration.

Let there be no misunderstanding: this was not exclusively a Patriot enclave, nor were Patriots the only ones to suffer. Loyalists comprised the majority of the population at the outset of the war and suffered greatly during it, though by contemporary accounts not as severely. Patriot homes were burned, but their enemies' homes and belongings were confiscated in much greater numbers. Loyalists and Patriots alike were carted off to captivity, although it was the British prisons in New York that have gone down in history as the most atrocious of the war, their reputations as hellholes unexaggerated. It was only the frequent prisoner exchanges that prevented a significant number of Patriot deaths in or caused by the prisons.

The countryside was transformed as well. Many areas of the place that was once described as a veritable Eden—a land of peace and plenty and the bounty of a diligent and prosperous people—would not be physically recognizable even a short time after the outbreak of the war. A Continental officer commented, "Our march was through the formerly delightful

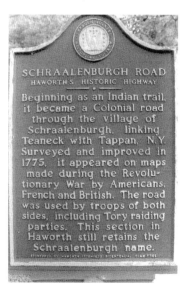

Historic marker on Schraalenburgh Road, Haworth. *Courtesy of Ira Lieblich.*

village of Schraalenburgh but was at the commencement of this Campaign reduced to a heap of rubbish." Neither could Bergen County's devastated residents any longer be called "the most Easie and Happy People of any Collony in North America."

Add to all of this the drought of 1779 that dried up the rivers needed to power the mills; the record-breaking, deadly severity of the winter of '79–'80; hunger, impoverishment and repeated foraging raids by both sides; and the picture is, in proportion, almost biblical. Fortunately, the plague of "pestilence"—the smallpox epidemic that raged in Massachusetts—didn't ravage the citizens of the neutral ground during the war, though it had been brought to Paulus Hook by British troops.

> *Samuel Demarest and his wife Margaritie Brinkerhoff Demarest lived in a large house about a mile south of the Closter Dock Road…Afraid of no one, local people told for years how he stood in the doorway of his house and defied [Lieutenant Colonel Abraham] Van Buskirk's men as they came up the Closter Road. They seized him as a prisoner, applied the torch to his house, killed his son Cornelius and wounded his son Hendrick.*
>
> *The women buried Cornelius' body near the farmhouse and watched Samuel Demarest, Cornelius Tallman, Jacob Cole, George Van Buskirk, Jeremiah Westervelt, and others carried off to prison in New York. Hendrick's life was saved only because one of the women of the household rushed to his rescue as he fell to the ground and boldly protected him from further injury.*
>
> *Captain John Huyler's company…arrived too late to do anything but save the cattle. The Tories burned the dwelling houses of Peter S. Demarest, Matthias Bogert, and Cornelius Huyler…Cornelius Bogert's, John Westervelt's and John Banta's barns were also destroyed. The raiders, a local man wrote, "were some of our Closter and Tappan old neighbors."*
>
> —*Leiby,* The Revolutionary War in the Hackensack Valley

The Civil War of the next century was in part a war between neighboring states. The war in the neutral ground was between neighboring families—and that made it personal. To some it became a matter of personal vengeance.

One wonders about the motives of Abraham Van Buskirk.

It is hard to square Van Buskirk's earlier appointment as a deputy representing Bergen County at the Provincial Congress at Trenton in May 1775 and his acceptance of a commission as surgeon for the Patriot militia with what he soon became: the most infamous and reviled Tory leader in the county and beyond. The minor plundering of his house at New Bridge at the time of Heath's December 1776 raid of Hackensack doesn't seem adequate to explain it; nor would, as some have suggested, the fact that the Lutheran Van Buskirk stood outside the prevailing Jersey Dutch society and may have been fixedly contemptuous of it. As lieutenant colonel with the Loyalist Fourth Battalion, New Jersey Volunteers, he was best known for his cruelty and the vigilante acts of his recruits. Notwithstanding newspaper accounts embellishing the numbers of Van Buskirk's raiders, and probably the catalogue of their violations as well, so extreme were some of his garrison's actions against the civilians of Bergen County that a high-ranking Tory, Peter DuBois, expressed shock and condemnation. He described, in a letter, a raid for which he cited Van Buskirk's responsibility as "a scene marked by circumstances of savage barbarity." He wrote that he saw "no reason to bring the horrors of war to the defenseless inhabitants of the neutral ground who were not engaged in warfare," and that perpetrators of the depraved acts "breathe nothing but fire and sword, and desolations—and those whom an ungovernable and rapacious soldiery have already plundered, they are for utterly destroying."

It is a wonder that anyone lived here, much less advertised their Patriotism. But reside and persevere they did. Why did they stay?

Though few were truly vociferous in their allegiance, here is a clue to the mindset of more than one outspoken Patriot: they risked all because they accepted that they would probably lose everything they possessed.

Why did the rest stay? Though initially no one had any idea that the war would last as long as it did, it was shortly clear that, whatever the duration, it was going to be less than unpleasant for those determined to stick it out. In both cases, partisan principle alone, fervent as it might have been, could not conceivably have been enough to motivate them to remain under such intolerable conditions. For Patriots, possible loss of their home lands was an, if not *the*, issue. In southernmost Bergen County, there were people living on land that had been in their families for as many as 125 years. In the rest of the county, as well as the Tappan, New York area, many families had been settled and had proliferated for a century. For a huge portion of the population, removing themselves to safer locales meant leaving the nexus of a huge extended family, including networks of families related by marriage. Nearly all of these inhabitants had Dutch ancestry. By their long history and their continuing majority in the Hackensack Valley, they could claim it as their own; because it held everything and everyone they held dear, it claimed and bound them tight.

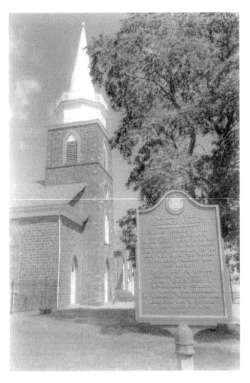

Historic marker for Church-on-the-Green (First Reformed Church), Hackensack. *Courtesy of Ira Lieblich.*

Indeed, according to wartime tax lists, the face of the neutral ground was overwhelmingly "Jersey Dutch," that misleading term for the amalgam of nationalities that had at some point intermarried with the Dutch settlers or otherwise been absorbed into their culture, bringing French, German, Swiss, Polish, Danish, English, Scottish and Italian surnames into the mix. Their cultural and social fabric was tightly woven by religion, marriage, decades or more of neighborly cohabitation and collective labor, lifestyle, language and even architecture. That the Dutch did not believe in primogeniture usually meant estate divisions among multiple siblings. This created large clusters of families of the same surname, and those immediately related, all over the area. They literally took up most of the inhabited space.

Agreed that the Jersey Dutch made up the majority, but judging from the lists of postwar Patriot claims for restitution filed with the new government, they seem to have been victimized disproportionately more. Why? It might have been different had Jersey Dutch Patriots not been branded by virtue of their affiliations with certain congregations in the Dutch Reformed Church. The schism that had begun three-quarters of a century earlier in the church in America, pitting progressives advocating home rule in religious matters against conservatives who insisted that control remain with the mother church in the Netherlands, oddly foretold later political alliances: "rebel" Patriots versus "loyalist" Tories. In fact, with very few exceptions, when sides were taken at the outset of the war, Coetus and Conferentie congregations split surgically along party lines. Jersey Dutch Patriots were self-advertised easy pickings for rampaging Tories. What had been a contentious ideological split progressed to political fracture, and eventually to malevolence and violence from the outset of the Revolution.

> *But they went on electing rebel legislatures and rebel judges as if they had been sovereign and independent since the time of William the Conqueror. More than self-interest moved these stubborn men; little wonder the frustrated British burned their courthouses and their homes.*
> —*Leiby*, The Revolutionary War in the Hackensack Valley

Despite pleas, little help came from the Continental army, whose commanders were chiefly interested in using the western shore of the Hudson as a vantage point from which to spy and keep protective eyes on the Highlands troops. Though they would eventually come late to the party, they otherwise abandoned the neutral ground to the homegrown militia (in their common view, a collection of hapless farmers). General McDougal, reporting to Washington on the battering of Closter, offered his view that fortifying the meager encampment of troops at Paramus was a waste of his men and that the beleaguered citizens of eastern Bergen County, a few miles away, were "too remote to help." His recommendation drew this response from Washington: "For the present I shall only say that I would not distress the posts under your command in order to cover that part of the country." Washington encouraged the militia to patrol the Closter area and to supply any useful intelligence, apparently willing to profit by them but not commit any splinter of the army to their rescue.

The militia was repeatedly demoralized by its abandonment and abjectly frustrated with its own inability to blanket the county with protection. It is truly a testament to its members and leadership that the companies of the Bergen County militia both persisted and increased their numbers as the war progressed.

Some of the stories of those who served border on the unbelievable. In his pension application, militiaman Daniel Vansciver testified to having enlisted and reenlisted in various companies at least *fifteen* times over six years of service.

Such were the heroes: the indefatigable, steadfast militia; everyday citizens—the tenacious, the believers, the defiant; our native Continentals (excepting their forages); the stalwart and single-minded provisional government. Hundreds of people to honor and remember…if only we would.

But he that shall endure unto the end, the same shall be saved.
Matthew 24:13

Then there were the aftershocks of the war.

Tory neighbors who did not emigrate returned to live among the exhausted, soul-sick Patriots and neutrals. Claims submitted to the new government for compensation for lost property resulted in nothing. Pensions for the Continental army and militias were not voted by Congress until 1832, when many of those who had served were long dead.

But the people rebuilt their lives and homes, settling down to unaccustomed peaceful days.

In the onrush of the formation of a national identity, the Jersey Dutch drew their culture around them like a blanket and, despite constant buffeting by change, religious and secular, the culture and language (an important unifier) persisted well into the twentieth century. They found at least a measure of contentment in this and peace in their connection with the past.

Patriot victory assuaged fears, but the page was slow in turning.

The outcome was grand—a resounding victory for the ages—but the process had been devastating. The toll in human spirit was immensely greater than in numbers of lives. "Men's souls" had not merely been "tried"; they had been battered for their lifetimes. The social fabric had nearly been destroyed. Fractures within families had an effect that would reverberate down through the generations.

It may not be the terrible untaught story that makes the war in the neutral ground significant to the outcome of the Revolution. The War for Independence might have been lost in Bergen County on November 20, 1776, had things happened just a little differently. Though it could not have been won here that day, the war might not have been won in the long run if not for the Retreat to Victory.

The story of triumph and independence is one for the posterity, one of a nation. The story of the wartime neutral ground is one that is profoundly our own.

———•———

Nancy Terhune is a twelfth-generation resident of Bergen County, descendant of many of the county's earliest settlers. She is a former trustee and vice-president of the Bergen

Nancy Terhune

County Historical Society and the Ridgewood Historical Society and the author-editor of Family Records of Northern New Jersey and Southern New York, 1624–1900: Original Genealogies of Our Ancestors. *Terhune is a marketing consultant and a writer and speaker on history and genealogy topics. She lives in a National Historic Landmark in Bergen County.*

"Had all the Cavalry been in the front...not one man could have escaped..."

Hopperstown, New Jersey, April 16, 1780

John U. Rees

Paramus, New Jersey, and the associated community of Hopperstown had been intermittently occupied by Continental or militia forces since December 1776, but not until 1780 did any serious military conflict occur there. The first clash took place on March 23, 1780, when two detachments of Crown troops attempted to capture and destroy the Continental army post at Paramus, one column crossing the Hudson, coming ashore at Closter Landing and advancing from there, with a second column moving from the southeast, via Hackensack village, which they plundered. The joint attack did not succeed in carrying the American post, and British and German troops involved were harried during their retreat by Whig regulars and militia.

From its beginning, the war had been one of neighbor against neighbor, brother against brother, and nowhere was this more evident than in northern New Jersey. One reason for the American post at Hopperstown, and part of the British desire to eradicate it, was the so-called London Trade, whereby local "disaffected" inhabitants supplied much-needed goods to British-held New York. Continental forces in the area were intended to interdict that trade and protect local Whigs, whereas the British high command certainly wanted to extend its control over the region.

After the March attempt, American troops centered at Hopperstown remained a thorn in the side of British and Loyalist forces. Consistent with established practice, the commanders and detachments manning Hopperstown and its satellites were regularly rotated. The post commander, "Majr. Anderson" (likely Archibald Anderson of the Third Maryland Regiment), was relieved by Major Thomas Lambert Byles of the Third Pennsylvania, on April 4, 1780.

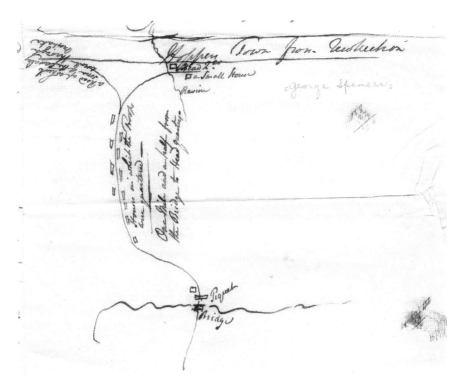

Map of attack on Hopperstown, New Jersey, April 16, 1780, enclosed in George Spencer to John G. Simcoe, undated, Simcoe Papers. 1774–1824, William L. Clements Library, University of Michigan. *Courtesy of Clements Library.*
Captions on map are as follows
Road across top of map: "Hopperstown from Weehawken."
Top right: Two buildings across ravine marked: "Head Q[uarte]rs" and "a Small House."
Top left: Left-hand road fork marked "a Road up which some of the Cavalry went through mistake."
Middle portion of map, with rows of houses on each side of road, marked: "Houses in which the Troops were quartered—One Mile and a half from the Bridge to Head quarters."
Bottom of map shows the river with position of the bridge and picket post.

On April 16, British forces struck again, this time with a straightforward, lightning assault. A number of units took part in the raid: Queen's Rangers Hussars (light cavalry), elements of the Seventeenth British light dragoons, Diemar's Hussars, Loyal American Regiment, Lieutenant William Stewart's Staten Island Volunteers (Loyalist light dragoons), German Jägers (light infantry), von Bose and von Mirbach Regiments.

The Queen's Rangers Hussars played a prominent role in the affair, and some discussion of their origin and organization is in order. The unit, composed of both infantry and cavalry, was first formed in August 1776 from Loyalists recruited in New York and Connecticut, and with men from the Queen's Loyal Virginia Regiment. In the winter of 1778–79, the Hussars were reorganized, "The Commander in Chief [Lieutenant General Sir Henry Clinton] intending to augment the Huzzars of the Queen's Rangers, to a troop of fifty, or more, Lieutenant Colonel [John Graves] Simcoe applied…that Lieutenant [Alexander] Wickham should be captain; Lieutenant [Allan] M'Nab lieutenant; Quarter–master [George] Spencer, of the Sixteenth dragoons, cornet; and Serjeant Spurry, of the same regiment, quartermaster." The Hussars were left behind at Richmond, Staten Island, New York, when Lieutenant Colonel Simcoe and the Queen's Ranger infantry embarked for Charleston, South Carolina, on April 7, 1780.

The Queen's Rangers' Captain Wickham's account of the April 16 Hopperstown attack was endorsed by Simcoe, who noted, "[Major] General [Wilhelm von] Knyphausen, by frequent and well–concerted expeditions, had kept the rebels fully employed in… the Jersies. On one of these attempts, the Huzzars of the Rangers were eminently distinguished, as was detailed to Lieutenant Colonel Simcoe by Captain Wickham."

Continental army regimental officer, circa 1780, wearing his sword at his waist and carrying an espontoon. The latter weapon replaced the light muskets (fusils) carried by many American officers earlier in the war. *Painting by Don Troiani, www.historicalimagebank.com.*

Here is the captain's report, including some clarifications from the statement of Queen's Rangers' Cornet George Spencer:

> *On the 15th of April, the cavalry on Staten Island, consisting of Cornet* [Thomas] *Tucker and twenty of the 17th regiment, light dragoons, Capt. Wickham with his troop of forty-five men, and Capt.* [Friedrich von] *Deimar with his huzzars, forty men crossed at Cole's ferry, and marched to English neighbourhood.*

(Diemar's unit consisted of German soldiers captured at Saratoga who escaped and returned to New York in summer 1778.)

Cornet Spencer noted they reached English Neighborhood at 1:00 a.m., "without being discovered," where, as Captain Wickham recalled, the cavalry "joined Major [Johann Christian] Du Buy [Regiment von Bose], with three hundred of the regiment De Bose and fifty of Colonel [Beverley] Robinson's corps [the Loyal American Regiment]." Spencer also stated that "the Order of march was—An advance Guard of the Q[ueen's]. Rangers, six men commd. by Serjt. McLaughlin, the Dragoons of the 17th, the Hessian Infantry & then the remainder of the Cavalry." Captain Wickham continues, "At New-Bridge Serjeant M'Laughlin [Wickham's Company], with six of the Rangers in advance, fell in with and either killed or took the whole of a small rebel out-post. The detachment then continued their march, leaving fifty infantry for the security of the bridge." According to Cornet Spencer, the "rebel out-post" at New Bridge consisted "of a Captain and thirty men."

Of this juncture, Spencer recorded,

> *An Hour after Daylight they reached Hoppers Town where two Hundred and fifty men were quartered Under Col. Bailey* [actually Major Thomas Lambert Byles]—*His Patrols had been out and returned—at the entrance of the Town there is a Bridge/there a picquet of a subaltern* [officer] *and twenty men were posted…Within a Mile of the Picquet Colo. DeBuy Informed <u>all</u> the Officers of Cavalry that such a picquet was posted there, with the exact situation of the Rebel troops.*

Captain Wickham's narrative continues:

> *At a convenient distance from Hopper Town, Major Du Buy gave his last orders for his surprise of* [Major Byles], *with three hundred rebels, posted at that place: the major was particularly attentive to a minute description of their situation. Cornet Spencer with twelve ranger huzzars, and Cornet Tucker with the like number of the 17th regiment to support him, made a general advance guard; then followed Capt. Diemar with his troop: the infantry and the remainder of the cavalry closed the rear. Hopper Town is a straggling village, more than a mile long; nearest, a court-house which contained an officer's piquet of twenty men, and which, if properly disposed, covered a bridge over which the troops must pass. The advance was ordered to force the bridge, and to push forward at full speed, through the town, to head quarters: this they effected after receiving an ineffectual fire from the picquet and from*

some of the windows: the rest of the cavalry dispersed, to pick up the fugitives and to take possession of the rebel's quarters, now abandoned. Cornet Spencer, on his arrival at his post with six men only, the rest not being able to keep up, found about five and twenty men drawn up on the road, opposite him, and divided only by a hollow way and small brook, with Hopper's house on their right, and a strong fence and swamp on their left. The officer commanding them [Major Byles]…talked to his men and asked his officers, "Shall we fire now or take possession of the house;" the latter was agreed on. The house was of stone, with three windows below and two above: at the moment of their going in, Cornet Spencer with his party augmented to ten of his own, and by two of the 17th regiment, passed the ravine, and taking possession of the angles of the house, ordered some of his men to dismount and to attempt to force one of the windows. Some [officers'] servants from a small out-house, commenced a fire: Corporal Burt [of Wickham's Company] with three men was sent to them, who broke the door open and took nine prisoners.

Then, as Cornet Spencer explained, "I attempted to speak to the people in the 1st House to offer them quarters if they would surrender but they had so many officers and were so well posted at the windows and knowing the House to be stone would not Answer otherwise than with shot."

We return to Captain Wickham's narrative:

They kept up a continual fire: finding it impossible to break the door open, which was attempted, and a man wounded through it, or to force any of the windows, he ordered fire to be brought from the out-house, with which he set one angle of the roof, which was of wood [shingles], in flames: he again offered them quarter if they would surrender; they still refused, though the flames were greatly increased. By this time some of the speediest of the cavalry had come to his assistance: the firing ceased. Captains Deimar and Wickham, &c., who had collected a great number of prisoners, and left some few men to guard them, until the infantry should come up, now joined the advance. [Major Byles] as he opened the door to surrender, was unfortunately shot by one of Captain Deimar's huzzars, and died three days after. Of the advance guard two men and three horses were killed, and two men and two horses wounded: one man and one horse of the 17th regiment were also killed. In this house…[the major], two captains, three subalterns, and twenty-one soldiers were taken. In the whole, twelve officers, with one hundred and eighty-two men were made prisoners. The party returned by the same route they had advanced, with little opposition and no loss. The plan of this expedition was well laid, and as well executed: Major Du Buy seemed to be master of the country through which he had to pass, and was well seconded by Capt. Deimar. Major Du Buy was pleased to honour the huzzars of the Rangers with his particular thanks and approbation. The house was well defended, and the death of the gallant [Major Byles] *was very much regretted by his opponents.*

Given his active role, George Spencer's closing words are compelling.

Never was a House better defended—[Major Byles] *was wounded in the Breast of which he died three days after—two men were killed and one wounded in the House by the shots from my men outside and notwithstanding the precaution I had taken of taking them close to the wall they killed two men and two Horses of the Q. Rangers and one of the 17ᵗʰ with his Horse—Wounded two men & one Horse of Mine—the* [major]…*Had all the Cavalry been in the front it would have been better—And I believe not one man could have escaped—but the road was narrow and the Hessians Could not move out of their way so fast as was necessary.*
The Hessians embarked for York Island at fort Lee.
We got safe to Staten Island.
The bravery of my Corporal Burt I must not forget.
The Commander in Chief returned thanks to the Corps.
DeBuy to the Rangers in particular.

Captain Jonathan Hallett, Second New York Regiment and commander at Paramus following the raid, notified General George Washington the same day:

Paramus April 16ᵗʰ 1780
Sir

It is with Regret I am under the Necessity of informing your Excellency of an Attack made by the Enemy this morning on the Detachment at this place…Our loss is Majr Byles badly wounded and prisoner on Parole Captains [Jacob] *Weaver* [10ᵗʰ Pennsylvania] *&* [Isaac] *Seely* [5ᵗʰ Pennsylvania] [1ˢᵗ] *Lieuts Briston* [Samuel Bryson, 7ᵗʰ Pennsylvania] *&* [James] *Glentworth* [6ᵗʰ Regiment] *of the Pensylvania Line Ensigns* [Nathaniel] *Thatcher* [Jackson's Additional Regiment] *&* [Henry] *Sherman* [Sherburne's Additional Regiment] *Genl Starks Brigade made prisoners 50 Non Commissd Officers & Privates missing 3*

A party of Hussars from the Loyalist Queen's Rangers Regiment advancing through hostile territory, reminiscent of the environs of Hopperstown, New Jersey, in April 1780. *Painting by Don Troiani, www.historicalimagebank.com.*

Privates wounded & one Killed we have lost likewise twenty five Men by Desertion out of the Commd. Nine of which left us last evening the Majr had Detachd two subalterns with thirty Men in pursuit of them.

Before we had Collected our Force the enemy retird / we immediately fell upon their rear [and] pursued them 12 Miles keeping up the whole time a very brisk fire on their flanks and rear Guard...The Militia behav'd very well on the Occasion the Officers and Men that was so fortunate as to escape being made prisoners Acted with the greatest Spirit—The Enemy have burned two Houses & a Mill the property of the Hoppers at this place with all our Provisions. Our Ammunition is Chiefly expended.

As with the March 23 Paramus attack, the newspapers spread word of Hopperstown. The most complete Continental account appeared in the *New Jersey Journal*, "Chatham, May 17," providing some new details of the action:

On the 16th ult. A detachment of two hundred continental troops...stationed at Paramus, was suddenly attacked by a party of the enemy...The attack commenced a little after sun-rise. Major Byles, besides his usual patroles, had that morning sent out two parties, each with a commissioned officer; but such is the situation of that part of the country, intersected with roads, and inhabited chiefly by disaffected people, that all precautions failed. His parties and patroles were eluded, and the sentinels near his quarters were the first that gave notice of the enemies approach. He had just paraded and dismissed his men. The advance of the horse was so rapid, that no time was left to reassemble them. The Major had no resource but the defence of the house he was in...He immediately made the best disposition the hurry of the moment would permit, and animated his men by his exhortation and example. A brisk fire ensued on both sides. The house was soon surrounded on every part, and no effort of the little party seemed capable of hindering the enemy from forcing their way. Some of the men, intimidated by so threatening a scene, began to cry for quarters; others, obeying the commands of their officers, continued to fire from the windows. The enemy without upbraided them with the perfidy of asking quarters and persisting in resistance; desiring them to come out and they would quarter them. Major Byles...in a determined tone, denied his having called for quarters; but his resolution could not avail, a surrender took place...in the act, the Major received a mortal wound in the left breast, with which, in two days after, he expired a victim to his gallantry and refined sense of duty...Lieutenants Glenworth and Sherman had thrown themselves in the Major's quarters, and assisted in the defence. They displayed great activity and bravery. The latter was wounded. Such part of the detachment as could be collected together, aided by a few spirited militia, hung close upon the rear of the enemy during their retreat, and harassed them with a continual fire, retaking four wagons with plunder and nineteen horses.

Lieutenant Bryson [7th Pennsylvania] *being a few days before detached by Major Byles with a small party to the New Bridge, defended that post for some time with great gallantry and coolness, he sustaining in person, with his espontoon, the attack of four horsemen, and received several wounds; but being overpowered with numbers, surrendered to one of their officers. It is said he received marks of politeness from them, on account of the great bravery and deliberate courage displayed by him during the skirmish.*

The enemy…plundered and burnt the house and mill of Mr. John Hopper, and that of his brother's. In the former the family of Mr. Abraham Brasher lived, who, with the rest, were left almost destitute of a second change of clothes. The commanding officer being requested by Mrs. Brasher on her knees to spare the house, he damn'd her, and bid her begone, declaring they all deserved to be bayoneted. They made their boast, that as Major Byles did not present the hilt of his sword in front, when surrendering, they shot him. Thus died this brave and gallant officer a victim to their savage cruelty.

The April 19 *Royal Gazette* gave additional information, including the presence of Lieutenant William Stewart's troop of Loyalist cavalry and a breakdown of Crown casualties.

New-York, April 19.
The following is published from good Authority.
Upon Saturday last the 15th inst. a cavalry detachment of about 120 men, composed of the 17th dragoons, Queen's Ranger Hussars, Diemar's Hussars, and Lieut. [William] *Stuart's* [light dragoon] *volunteers, drawn from Staten Island, with a body of 312 infantry, composed of 12 Jagers, 150 men of the regiment Bose, 100 men of the regiment Mirbach, and 50 men of the Loyal American Regiment, drawn from York Island; the whole under the command of Major Du Buy of the regiment of Bose, were landed in the Jersies, the cavalry near the extremity of Bergen Neck, the infantry near Fort Lee…*

Return of the killed, wounded and missing of the troops at the affair at Hopper's-town the 16th inst.
17th light-dragoons, 1 horse killed, 3 rank and file wounded, 1 horse wounded.
Queen's Ranger Hussars, 3 rank and file killed, 3 horses killed, one rank and file wounded, two horses wounded.

Diemar's hussars, 2 rank and file wounded, one horse wounded.

Staten Island volunteers, 2 rank and file wounded.

Jägers, 1 wounded.

Mirbach, 1 killed, 11 rank and file wounded.

Bose, 2 killed, 1 serjeant wounded, 5 rank and file wounded.

Loyal Americans, 1 killed, 5 wounded.

Total 7 rank and file killed, 4 horses killed, two serjeants wounded 29 rank and file wounded, four horses wounded.

Two wounded men left behind are included in the above return, many of the wounded are doing their duty.

"Revolutionist" participants left a number of old-age accounts of the affair. Some are brief, such as Bergen County militia Captain John Outwater's 1784 certificate: "Henry Denny whas a Soldier In my Company of Melitie of Bergen County Coln. Deys Regt. at the time he Got wounded By the British On an alarm In April 1780." In his pension deposition, Josiah Willard, Hastings's Company, Jackson's Massachusetts Regiment, merely mentioned the fact of his wounding on April 16, and that he was discharged after returning from captivity in November 1780.

Some men offered more details. Bergen militiaman Benjamin Romaine gives an idea of the hurly-burly Crown forces' advance and withdrawal:

I was…engaged throughout the whole day, when the enemy burned Paramus and Hopperstown, about Eight miles above new bridge. The troops harassed the rear and flanks of the enemy, in their march to the Hoppers Mills, and continued to do so, in their final retreat back to Fort Lee; at which place they recrossed the Hudson for fort Washington…we recaptured almost all the baggage and Effects which they had plundered. In the course of the conflict the enemy horse made three attempts of attack, on our several companies, pressing on their flanks and rear, but at no time did they come to a charge. On one occasion…they surprized about one hundred of us, in a clear field: they advanced at full speed and with apparent determination: we instantly formed, as retreat was useless, when the enemy declined the attack and filed off. Our officers, notwithstanding to the great mortification, forbid us to fire, though the enemy was at easy distance shot.

In 1860 nonagenarian Stephen Lutkins, who "now lives with his grand daughter's husband…very deaf & no teeth—so that it is not easy to talk with him," stated that he *well remembers the burning of Hoppertown—the same day a valuable dog belonging to his Father was shot by the british on their March up—about 1½ miles below said place. He well remembers the enemy being drove back by the Militia regiment and the Continental troops…the British were continually robbing and plundering the inhabitants, he well remembers how his mother buried the silver spoons finger rings &c. to avoid them being taken by the enemy.*

Some participants claimed another reason for singling out the Hopperstown post. Ninety-three-year-old Stephen Westervelt testified in 1860, "The British came out of New York & burned the property of Captain John Hopper…All the stores of the US Army were placed in custody at Hoppertown and consequently required a great amount of vigilence…& being a River County so near New York there was scarcely any respite." Peter Van Buskirk noted, "Hoppertown was a depot for the Arms stores &c of the American Troops, [and] Militia," while Mr. Lutkins stated, "Major Boyles and others with a Garrison and soldiers was quartered at Hoppertown and ammunition &c was stored therein this was a general Depot for the American Army."

In 1838 Mary Hopper, wife of Captain John Hopper, related her memories of the day and what it meant to her family:

On the 16th day of April 1780 a troop of Dragoons of British Light Horse surprised the American garison of soldiers stationed at Hoppertown, Killed the Maj[or] in Command took a few prisoners and burned and destroyed two Dwelling Houses one store House, & one Grist Mill with two [ton?] of stores…one of the Dwelling houses and Store House was the property of her late Husband [John Hopper] that in Consequence of the Destruction of the buildings, her late husband lost all his private… property Contained in the buildings, Consisting of Household furniture, a Large quantity of Linnen and various other goods, And also the sum of seven thousand Dollars in Money, Not a Dollar of Which Money was saved…The Money was put in a safe place in the house some time previous to its destruction by fire on the Morning of the 16 April 1780 at Dawn of Day…the Buildings Destroyed were wood and occupied by the American Troops, and Arms, Amunition, & provisions Kept and stored in the Buildings for the use of the American garison of Officers & soldiers quartered and stationed at Hoppertown…her late Husband Escaped at the time with the loss of his hat.

To some degree the Hopperstown enterprise gave the British the result they desired. On April 17, General Washington informed Congress, "I am sorry to be obliged to transmit the inclosed disagreeable account from Paramus. The Post there is intended to restrain the traffic between that part of the Country and New York which from the disposition of the Inhabitants has been very considerable. This consideration has induced me to station a party there though at some hazard, but…with reluctance I imagine I shall be obliged to withdraw it, for the extreme disaffection of the Inhabitants gives the Enemy even greater advantages than was supposed."

The region remained only intermittently protected for some time after the April 16 attack. French officer François Jean de Beauvoir, Marquis de Chastellux, noted,

> *The 23rd [November 1780] I set out at eight o'clock, with the intention of arriving in good time at the Marquis de la Fayette's camp…The shortest road was by Paramus; but my guide insisted on my turning to the northward, assuring me that the other road was not safe, that it was infested by tories, and that he always avoided it, when he had letters to carry.*

The translator, "an English gentleman, who resided in America at that period," supported Chastellux's narrative, writing,

> *The guide gave the Marquis very true information, for the Translator who took the Paramus road, had several well-founded alarms, in passing through that intricate country. At Hopper's Mill, near Paramus, where he slept among myriads of rats in a milk house, the family assured him, that their quarters were constantly beat up, and horses, men, &c. carried off. At this place there was no lock to the stable door, which they said was a superfluous article, as these banditti were guilty of every act of violence.*

Despite the setback, local Whigs were undaunted. This extremity of spirit is evident (perhaps with some hyperbole) in Benjamin Romaine's 1834 pension narrative:

> *I…here sketch my three or four…months service under my Brother, at the command of my Father in 1777. I had pleaded excuse from going to school, as my Father had requested, (we then lived on the lines where both the belligerant parties had alternate possession.) One evening my Father*

came into the house with a large english musket, and its appendages, with a catouch box filled with 24 rounds of ball catriges. He sat the musket in the closet; mother asked his meaning, he answered not. In the early morning he bid me rise, and buckled on me the armour, and said, "you have refused to make effort with me to perfect your education, now go to your Brother and defend your country!" These trying moments, Sir, to the family, can never cease to be appreciated, while a particle of life remains, and the effect of this command has never ceased to influence my life and conduct…and "in defence of my Country;" and very specially in support of its present united Constitution of general Government, and opposed to that venal tendency of State Sovereignty aberrations, as under the old Confederation, by whomsoever or in whatever form these may make appearance…These I shall never cease to oppose by every talent, and every remaining energy of my life…To resume. I proceeded to the liberty Pole [Bergen County, New Jersey] *to my Brothers quarters, was gazed uppon through the range of tory neighbourhood, it was exclaimed, that old Rebel has now also sent his youngest son to join his other son, at the liberty Pole.*

———•———

Special thanks to Todd W. Braisted and Donald Londahl-Smidt, without whose assistance and generosity this work would not have been possible.

The author's article on the March 23, 1780 action at Paramus, New Jersey, may be viewed online at http://tinyurl.com/bja36.

THE DESPERATE *HUIS VROUWS* OF REVOLUTIONARY BERGEN

CAROL KARELS

This country is in a miserable situation, the inhabitants afraid of every person they see.
—*Israel Shreve in a memo to George Washington about Bergen County, New Jersey, March 1778*

Remember the Ladies!" Abigail Adams wrote to her husband, John, in the summer of 1776 as he feverishly worked on the Constitution. Much has been written about Revolutionary War generals' wives such as Martha Washington, Catherine (Caty) Greene and Lucy Knox, who spent winters with their husbands in Morristown, Valley Forge and Middlebrook—how they knitted socks for the soldiers during the day and occasionally danced with the generals during the long, cold nights.

The letters of Abigail Adams and the poems of the slave poetess Phyllis Wheatley, all written during the Revolutionary War, reveal the story of the politics of the war from a woman's perspective. Cokie Roberts writes about the wives of the founding fathers in her book *Founding Mothers*.

Numerous books have also been written specifically about ordinary women during the Revolutionary War: *Revolutionary Mothers*, *The Women of '76*, *Liberty Belles* and *Ladies at the Crossroads* to name a few. They tell the stories of the Molly Pitchers, who provided water to the soldiers in battle; of women such as Deborah Sampson, who donned men's clothing and fought in battle; and of the camp followers on both sides who served as nurses, cooks, laundresses, seamstresses and more. But the stories of Bergen County women, with the exception of Theodosia Prevost of the

Hermitage, profiled in *The Revolutionary War in Bergen County: The Times that Tried Men's Souls*, and Firth Haring Fabend's novel *Land So Fair*, seem to have been forgotten.

Over one thousand men, with iconic Bergen County names such as Demarest, Zabriskie, Vreeland and Van Buskirk, are listed in the index of Adrien Leiby's definitive book, *The Revolutionary War in the Hackensack Valley*. Only five wives and widows are mentioned, yet the *huis vrouws* were just as affected by the war that came into their homes from November 20, 1776, to the war's end in 1783 as their men. They were held just as accountable for—and probably helped frame—the political decisions their husbands made. Unfortunately, the majority of their diaries and letters, if they had time to write them, have either not been saved, weren't translated from Jersey Dutch or were destroyed. From what we *do* know, the Revolutionary War years were trying times for women's souls too. A case can clearly be made that the *huis vrouws* of Bergen County, during the Revolutionary War, lived lives of desperation.

Before the Revolution, Bergen County had about three thousand inhabitants, most living in close proximity to the main roads in the area: the King's Highway (Grand Avenue), Kinderkamack Road and Paramus Road. Then, as today, it was one of the most diverse and prosperous places in the world. Most residents were fourth- or fifth-generation farmers of Dutch, English, French, Scots-Irish and Polish background, who spoke a mix of low Dutch and English (Jersey Dutch) in their homes and churches. They owned large farms filled with orchards, fields of wheat, vegetable gardens, sheep and cattle. They ran their farms with the help of slaves, who made up a fifth of the population.

"Hearty abundance" was one phrase prewar travelers used to describe Bergen County farms, most of which had large outbuildings, a spring-fed dairy barn, cider houses with a mill and press, tanning vats for leather making and orchards. Spinning wheels and butter churns were standard fixtures on the front porches. Visitors described it as a Garden of Eden.

The Jersey Dutch were frugal, industrious, neat, clean and unpretentious. Their culinary habits are one example of this. According to Leiby, the *huis vrouws* fed their men *sappaan* (cornmeal mush and milk) for supper every day, from cradle to death. Special meals might include mince pies, *rolletjes* (chopped beef and suet, seasoned and spiced, rolled up in tripe, boiled for a day and then served sliced), sausages, pumpkin *koondjes* and *kool slaa* (shredded cabbage in vinegar). Daughters and sons were educated in both English and Dutch but spoke Jersey Dutch at home and in church. Most attended the Dutch Reformed Church, the only organized church in the county, choosing either the reform Coetus congregation or the orthodox Conferentie congregation.

Before the war, the *huis vrouws* of Bergen County had a high degree of independence, more than their counterparts in other parts of America or Europe. To the shock of travelers from other areas, Bergen County women bridled and mounted their own horses, rode horses and drove horse-driven carts alone and rode in stagecoaches without escorts. In addition to household chores, they knew how to till the soil, harvest the crops, shoot a musket for self-protection and slaughter and cure the meat. Besides bearing children, they bared their legs, and visitors expressed shock that they wore (relatively) short frocks and went barefoot in the summer! Instead of wearing petticoats, they displayed their elaborately embroidered, colorful and multi-layered undergarments in the living rooms of their homes, the only source of decoration and a source of great pride.

Although married women could not legally own property (only spinsters and widows could), it was not uncommon for a woman to manage a family business, start her own or take over the family enterprise if her husband died. Among the businesses women owned in Bergen County were taverns, mills, shops and forges. *Huis vrouws* often took on the role of marketing the farm produce as well.

After the Boston Tea Party of 1773, Bergen County *huis vrouws* expressed their patriotism by rejecting British-made goods and forming "women's circles" and "bees" for spinning, weaving, sewing and quilting. Like other women in the colonies, they wanted to show they were self-sufficient and independent of Britain's cloth and textile industry. At such get-togethers, these Daughters of Liberty no doubt spoke about politics, their growing dedication to the Patriot cause and, perhaps, the Sons of Liberty.

It is highly unlikely, as these women wove and spun together, that they had any inkling that misery was coming—that their peaceful and prosperous valley would be overrun by two warring armies and roving bands of lawless cowboys for the next six years, that family life and businesses would be disrupted or destroyed, that once-plentiful goods would be scarce or prohibitively expensive, that diseases would take their toll among both civilian and military populations and their garden of Eden left desolate.

How could Loyalist wives foresee that, in the summer of 1776, their homes would be confiscated, their husbands seized and imprisoned in the Morristown Jail and they and their children sent to live in British-held

Reconstruction of soldiers' hut in Fort Lee Historic Park, Fort Lee. *Courtesy of Ira Lieblich.*

territory? And how could Patriot wives imagine that, just months later, after the British invasion of New Jersey, *their* homes would be stripped bare of beds, bedding and kitchen utensils by British and Hessian camp followers, or that their husbands, fathers and brothers would be seized from their farms and imprisoned in Manhattan's notorious Sugar House, often left to die from starvation, disease and neglect? How could any of these women imagine that close friendships, family ties and neighborly relations would be forever torn apart by acts of betrayal?

Yet the appearance of thirty thousand British and Hessian troops in New York Harbor in the summer of 1776 ushered in all that—six years of pure misery for Bergen County residents. The British offered protection to former Patriots who now signed loyalty oaths. For many residents, the decision to sign was based on a sheer desire to survive. But possession of the signed oaths didn't deter British and Hessian soldiers, and their camp followers, from looting and burning homes indiscriminately. The choice over which George to pledge allegiance to—King George III or George Washington—became increasingly more difficult, and loyalties frequently changed.

Linda Grant DePauw, author of *Fortunes of War: New Jersey Women and the Revolution*, wrote, "No matter what side they favored in the war, New Jersey women were generally reluctant for their husbands and sons to enlist. With the men away, who would plow the fields, chop the firewood, and harvest the crops?"

Most Bergen County Patriot men, for that reason, joined the militia instead of the Continental army. The army required months of service in other parts of the country; joining the militia meant they could farm by day, patrol the local neighborhood at night and be near their *huis vrouws*. Many Bergen County Loyalists, on the other hand, joined the Fourth Battalion, New Jersey Volunteers, also known as the Greencoats, led by former Patriot Abraham Van Buskirk.

"Families who lived along the main roads bore a special burden during the war," wrote Delight W. Dodyk in her essay "Troublesome Times A-Coming" in *New Jersey and the American Revolution*. Bergen County was one massive "road" located between the headquarters of both armies. Both armies, as well as small parties on special missions, crossed and recrossed it for the duration of the war. The area was known as "the neutral ground" because county government ceased functioning after the British invasion of 1776, and neither army officially protected the area. Patriot civilians and militiamen looked to Governor Livingston and the Council

Revolutionary War plate and utensil. *Courtesy of the Schoolhouse Museum, Ridgewood, New Jersey. Photograph courtesy of Ira Lieblich.*

of Safety for assistance. The council began to issue passes and conduct papers to those whose loyalty to the newly born State of New Jersey or to the Continental Congress was assured, but improper use of these passes hampered their success.

The county became a general scouting ground for British, Hessian and Continental soldiers, who went on foraging expeditions to feed their hungry men and horses, and the multitude of women and children that followed both armies known as camp followers. The women in the train of the Continental army were typically uprooted housewives following their husbands—preparing meals, doing laundry and other chores as was customary in nineteenth-century warfare. Besides prostitutes, among those who followed the British army were Loyalist widows and single women who had no other means of protecting or supporting themselves. They made money doing laundry and cooking for British soldiers, as well as receiving half rations. The Hessians had their women camp followers as well.

The Revolutionary War in Bergen County became as much a bitter civil war as a struggle for independence. The sides for whom the men chose to fight most often reflected the sides taken in a two-decades-long religious war that had begun in 1755, which resulted in a schism in the Dutch Reformed Church. The war of words that had begun in the churches of Bergen County a generation earlier had evolved into a war of revenge and retaliation, fought with intense viciousness. Politics were preached in the pulpit: Conferentie ministers argued for support of King George III; Coetus ministers rallied parishioners for liberty.

The result was that neighbors were pitted against neighbors, brothers against brothers and fathers against sons. Wives often had to deal with divided loyalties among their husbands, brothers and fathers. But their husbands' political choices determined their fate. Wealth or class, or whom you were related to, didn't matter.

While their men were away in prison, involved in local skirmishes, on night patrols or dead, the *huis vrouws* provided quarters for military officers in the neighborhood, dealt with starving stragglers from both armies who wandered through their property looking for food and shelter, nursed wounded soldiers from both sides, risked their lives to hide soldiers in their homes, gathered information while marketing their wares or engaged in illicit trade.

In time Bergen County became a no-man's land overrun with spies, deserters, runaway slaves and outlaw gangs who cut down fences and trees

Silk wedding slippers, circa 1782. *Courtesy of the Schoolhouse Museum, Ridgewood, New Jersey. Photograph courtesy of Ira Lieblich.*

for fuel and warmth, pillaged and plundered homes of possessions and conducted midnight terror raids.

Colonel Levi Pawling, of the Continental army, wrote, "The good people of Bergen County lay greatly exposed to both internal and external enemies." Avoiding misfortune and surviving each day was a major accomplishment. Their Garden of Eden had become a land of devastation, a Hell on earth.

Following war's end in 1783, Bergen County men spoke with bitterness about their experiences for years; many of their observations were recorded and later published in Leiby's book. But what of the personal stories of their wives, mothers and sisters?

John U. Rees's essay on the recollections of Helen Kortright Brasher, a New York City resident and wife of Colonel Abraham Brasher of the New York Militia, gives us insights into what it was like to live in exile in Bergen County during the war. With the exception of Firth Haring Fabend's novel *Land So Fair,* published in 2008, history seems to have forgotten the stories of the desperate *huis vrouws* who called Bergen County home during the Revolutionary War. Tragic tales of molestation, family betrayal, heroic acts of self-protection and decisions made under extreme duress seem to have gone to the grave with them.

Under such circumstances, it's highly unlikely that those women who owned land were celebrating their unique, if short-lived, right to vote (in New Jersey). Undoubtedly, they were more concerned about repairing their homes and getting life back to normal. Desperate widows sought to marry British and Hessian soldiers who had deserted, seeking a second chance at life in a new country filled with freedom and hope. In time, some exiled Loyalists returned to Bergen County. Homes and barns were rebuilt, trees replanted and rocky relationships with former neighbors and family members restored or set aside. With the eventual return of peace and prosperity, these women's stories evaporated and became more forgotten history.

———•———

Carol Karels is an author, public speaker, public relations consultant and a former ER nurse. She has written four books on Leonia history, is the editor of The Revolutionary War in Bergen County: The Times that Tried Men's Souls *(The History Press, 2007) and is the author of* Cooked: An Inner City Nursing Memoir, *which won an American Journal of Nursing Book of the Year award in 2005. She has also written travel books on Greece and Bulgaria. She is a graduate of Chicago's Cook County Hospital School of Nursing and has a degree in history from the University of Illinois.*

The Zabriskies:

A Bergen County Family Feud

Joseph Suplicki

This is a story of the Zabriskie family's divided loyalties during the Revolutionary War. Similar stories could be found in many of the old Jersey Dutch families in the area. The seeds of disagreement had been sown years earlier by a schism in the Dutch Reformed Church over the idea of training and ordaining ministers here in the colonies, rather than in Holland—or, of European rule versus home rule. The Coetus-Conferentie schism eventually divided many families in Bergen County.

The Bridge that Saved a Nation (as New Bridge can be considered) reminds us of just how close to home the differences between families were before, during and even after the American Revolution. On the west side of the Hackensack River stood the home, mills and farm of John Zabriskie. Across the bridge on the east side of the river was the farm of Dr. Abraham Van Buskirk. As we shall see, the Bridge that Saved a Nation spanned the Hackensack River between the lands of two men who, at the beginning of hostilities, were both prominent citizens and apparent Patriots. But events proved them to be ardent Loyalists, both eventually serving as officers in the king's army. And each had his properties confiscated by the State of New Jersey.

Our family in question is that of Jan Zaborowkij, the second son of Albert Zaborowskij, progenitor of the Zabriskie family, who were originally from Poland. Jan had six sons and two daughters. Of three sons and the daughters, not enough is known of their whereabouts or loyalties to judge them. But two sons, and the son and a grandson of another, figure in our story.

The sons are Peter and Joost on one side, and son Jan J.'s son John and grandson John, his daughter Elizabeth Seaman's husband and sons on the

Old photo postcard of the Mansion House/Peter Zabriskie's House, Hackensack. *From the collection of Barbara Marchant.*

other. With four generations of Jan or John, following the custom of the times, each time the oldest John died, his son, known until then as John Jr., became John, and his son became John Jr. Or, in other words, at some point in their lives, three were known as John Zabriskie Jr.

On the Patriot side: Peter Zabriskie, born 1721, lived in Hackensack near the courthouse. His house became known as the Mansion House, used as a tavern and hotel. He was a justice or freeholder of Bergen County many times from 1754 to 1776, and freeholder again in 1788. On March 23, 1780, he was captured during a British raid on Hackensack and taken to the Sugar House Prison in New York City. Available records do not indicate how long he was imprisoned there, before most likely being exchanged for a British prisoner held by the Continentals. He was one of the three Bergen County delegates to sign New Jersey's ratification of the Constitution of the United States on December 19, 1787.

Joost Zabriskie, born in 1727, built a home on River Road in Teaneck, a short distance south of Cedar Lane, in either 1751 or 1761, on land originally owned by his grandfather. He served as freeholder of Bergen County in 1774, 1783 and 1784. Because he lived near often-raided Hackensack, he had considerable property taken or destroyed by the British between 1776 and September 1778. On August 6, 1777, he testified before the Council of Safety of the State of New Jersey about the "disaffection" of his nephew

Old photo postcard showing the Steuben House, River Edge. *From the collection of Barbara Marchant.*

John Zabriskie, and on October 11, 1783, he appeared before the mayor of New York City to sign a deposition as to the value of his nephew's property when confiscated.

On the Loyalist side: Jan J. Zabriskie, born approximately in 1716, had purchased the property on the west side of the Hackensack River from Johannes Ackerman in 1745 and built the oldest part of the Steuben House in 1752.

Jan J. Zabriskie had two children, twins John and Elizabeth, born in 1741. Elizabeth married Edmund Seaman in 1768 at Schraalenburgh, and died in New York City in March 1774, shortly after the birth of her third son.

Jan J. Zabriskie died in September or October 1774, mentioning in his will his wife, Annatje, son John and grandchildren John, Benjamin and Edmund Seaman, children of his deceased daughter. Named as executors were his wife Annatje, son John, son-in-law Edmund Seaman and Joost Zabriskie (undoubtedly his brother). The lands mentioned were the farm on the east side of the Hackensack River, lands on Long Cripple Bush Creek and Slokeup. The "house where I live, the mills and the whole farm thereunto belonging, with the appurtenances," were left to his son John Zabriskie.

Following the closing of the port of Boston in the spring of 1774, the freeholders and people of Bergen County held a meeting at the County Courthouse on June 25, chaired by Justice Peter Zabriskie. The freeholders were Isaac Van Der Beck, Nicausie Terhune, Hendrick Kuyper, John Van Horne, John Benson, Joost Zabriskie, Albert Ackerman, James Board, Edo Merseles and Hendrick Doremus.

At this point, since they were still hopeful of reconciling their grievances with England, the meeting produced the following preamble and resolutions, which were signed by 328 citizens of Bergen County:

> *This meeting being deeply affected with the calamitous condition of the inhabitants of Boston in the province of Massachusetts Bay, in consequence of the late Act of Parliament for blocking up the port of Boston, and considering the alarming tendency of the Act of the British Parliament for the purpose of raising a revenue in America.*
>
> *Do Resolve,*
>
> *1st. That they think it their greatest happiness to live under the government of the illustrious House of Hanover, and that they will steadfastly and uniformly bear true and faithful allegiance to His Majesty King George the Third under the enjoyment of their constitutional rights and privileges.*
>
> *2nd. That we conceive it to be our indubitable privilege to be taxed only by our own consent, given by ourselves or by our representatives; and that we consider the Acts of Parliament declarative of their right to impose internal taxes on the subjects of America as manifest encroachments on our national rights and privileges as British subjects, and as inconsistent with the idea of an American Assembly or House of Representatives.*
>
> *3rd. That we will heartily unite with this Colony in choosing delegates to attend a general congress from the several provinces of America in order to consult on and determine some effectual method to be pursued for obtaining a repeal of the said Acts of Parliament, which appear to us evidently calculated to destroy that mutual harmony and dependence between Great Britain and her colonies which are the basis and support of both.*
>
> *And we do appoint Theunis Dey, John Demarest, Peter Zabriskie, Cornelius Van Vorst, and John Zabriskie, Jr., Esquires, to be a committee for corresponding with the committees of the other counties in this Province, and particularly to meet with the other county committees at New Brunswick, or such other place as shall be agreed upon, in order to attend the general congress of delegates of the American Colonies for the purpose aforesaid.* [Two-fifths of the committee being from our family.]

A Committee of Safety was organized, chaired by John Fell, a devoted Patriot of Paramus (now Allendale).

However, following events in Lexington and Concord in April 1776, and the response in Philadelphia in July, it became time for the colonists to declare their loyalties.

Nothing of consequence occurred in Bergen County until early in 1776, when word was received that Lord Howe was on his way to New York. Three companies from Bergen were raised and joined in battalion with three from Essex and two from Burlington, under Colonel Philip Van Cortland, Lieutenant Colonel David Brearley and Major Richard Dey. The regular militia of Bergen County was organized in one regiment with the following officers: Theunis Dey of Preakness (the Dey Mansion in Wayne), colonel; John Zabriskie of New Bridge (the Steuben House), lieutenant colonel; Richard Dey of Preakness (son of Colonel Dey), captain, first major; John Mauritius Goetchius of Bergen (Jersey City), captain, second major; George Ryerson, adjutant; and Dr. Abraham Van Buskirk of Teaneck, surgeon. Our New Bridge men made up one-third of the officers of this militia.

However, on June 16, 1776, John Zabriskie resigned his commission and changed his allegiance to the king. On August 6, 1777, he was charged with "disaffection" by his uncle, Joost Zabriskie. He fled behind British lines in 1780 and became a "half-pay Captain" of the British forces. His lands were confiscated by the State of New Jersey in 1781 and given to Baron von Steuben. In 1784 and again in 1790, he submitted a claim to the British government for financial redress for his losses through confiscation. His brother-in-law, Edmund Seaman, who resided in New York City, also had his Bergen County lands confiscated. Interestingly, after the war John returned to Bergen County, along with his son and at least one of his nephews. His son, John Zabriskie Jr., purchased the family estate on December 4, 1788, from Baron von Steuben for £1,200, New York money.

In 1791, ten years after having his property confiscated, John J. Zabriskie was back in New Bridge, taxed on thirty acres, two gristmills and one slave. His son, John Zabriskie Jr., was listed as a householder and merchant, and his nephew John Seaman owned one vessel.

Of importance both before and during the retreat across New Bridge was General Washington's stay at the Mansion House of Peter Zabriskie. Washington was there when word was received of the invasion from the north. The general raced to Fort Lee, ordering an evacuation of the fort and the retreat across New Bridge. He spent the night in Hackensack at the Mansion House and left the next morning to lead the retreat through

New Jersey into Pennsylvania. Following the war, Peter Zabriskie sold land in Hackensack to the county opposite the Mansion House for a new courthouse to replace the original, which had been burned by the British in 1780.

Following the November 1776 retreat across New Bridge, Dr. Abraham Van Buskirk also resigned his commission and was appointed lieutenant colonel to head the Fourth Battalion, New Jersey Volunteers, which in July 1781 became the Third Battalion, after the Second Battalion was disbanded and drafted into the Third and Fourth with subsequent renumbering. Dr. Van Buskirk became known as "Buskirk the Butcher" and would be blamed for most of the atrocities inflicted by any Loyalist troops in the Bergen County area. In September 1781, the new Third Battalion joined the expedition under Brigadier General Benedict Arnold to New London. Unlike John Zabriskie, Van Buskirk never returned to New Bridge. After the war he received half-pay for life and land in Nova Scotia, and he became the first mayor of Shelburne, Nova Scotia. His son, Jacob, who had been a captain in his father's battalion, also moved to Nova Scotia and received land and half-pay for life.

Joseph Suplicki, a Ridgewood native, is a member of the Ridgewood Historic Preservation Commission, former president and trustee of the Genealogical Society of Bergen County and currently a trustee of the Ridgewood Historical Society. Joe and his wife, Peggy Norris, are co-historians for the Village of Ridgewood. He is a descendant of the first white child born in New Netherland, Sarah Rapelje; four of the five sons of Albrecht Zaborowskij; and an eleventh- or twelfth-generation resident of Bergen County, with ties to numerous other early Bergen County families.

The Revolutionary Roadways
of Bergen County

Benjamin Rubin

If we recall pivotal battles in American history, location likely comes
to mind. Gettysburg. The Alamo. The Battle of Lexington and
Concord. When recalling these decisive moments of history, locations
are remembered, but the names of instrumental roadways are frequently
forgotten. Yet roads are significant contributors to the outcome of a battle,
even perhaps a war. Unlike roads of the past, roads of the present are
easily recalled: a trip down New Bridge Road for dinner, or a drive on
Closter Dock Road to run an errand. Several of the roads in Bergen
County that are traveled upon today served people during the time of the
American Revolution. Now, as in the past, these roads remain critical for
the successful movement of people and commerce.

This essay examines the history of roads in Bergen County and investigates
their significance in the American Revolution. We begin by detailing
methods of travel in Bergen County and how roads were constructed
leading up to the Revolution. After explaining road conditions, the way
that roads were utilized in the Revolution is explored. Specific emphasis is
placed on learning about the vital role that roads played in the Americans'
retreat from Fort Lee. Strategies employed by the Americans and British
on the roads in Bergen County are considered. After detailing the roads'
Revolutionary past, present uses are explored. The Bergen County
Historical Society (BCHS) Historic Sites Marker Program, which is also
known casually as "The Blue Marker Program," is detailed. We conclude
by questioning how roads from the Revolution should be remembered in
Bergen County today.

Historic marker on Closter Dock Road, Alpine. *Courtesy of Ira Lieblich.*

Around the time of the American Revolution, methods other than road travel dominated transportation. In *The Long Retreat*, Arthur Lefkowitz explains that land near the Hackensack River held a higher value because "the rivers surpassed the primitive roads as the best routes of travel." The primary movement of commerce ran along rivers instead of roads. A lack of developed roads impeded traditional military organization. Lefkowitz asserts that because of poor conditions, "it was far easier to support local militia for a few days or weeks than any sizable and continuously operating national army in the field." This example highlights that the roads of the Revolution were a determining factor in the formation of both military and strategy.

Roads that did exist in colonial America were modeled after the British concept that each county court was responsible for building and maintaining its roads. At the time of the Revolution, the residents of Bergen County would have been hard-pressed to brag about their roads' conditions. West of Fort Lee the only roads in existence were narrow farm lanes. Farmers in Bergen County helped to improve roads in their district as a way of working off road tax. Anyone not dutifully completing his work was fined one dollar. This penalty was not enough to prevent workers from digging roadside ditches and throwing dirt into the center of the roadbed. Although this construction sufficed temporarily, each big storm washed away the dirt. These mud roads of Bergen County had varying conditions depending on the season. A dry summer created an unpleasant dust in the air and strong spring rains flooded the roads.

Prior to the Revolution, the main motivation for constructing roads was to transport produce from New Jersey farms to river ports so that produce could be shipped to nearby cities. Before the war began, farmers likely lacked the knowledge that they were assisting in constructing roads that would be used for war. Once the Revolutionary War entered Bergen County, roads became a dynamic element of the war. One example of the importance

British Scaling the Palisades. Illustration by permission of Gray's Watercolors, grayswatercolors@rcn.com.

of roads can be understood by the events that unfolded when the British attacked Fort Lee. Many historians assert that if the British had captured the Americans after taking Fort Lee, the war would have soon been over. Roads were certainly not the only reason for the Americans' successful retreat, but roads did play a critical role in the escape.

George Washington found himself frustrated with the road conditions of Bergen County. Prior to the British attack on Fort Lee, he ordered supplies to be moved farther into the interior of New Jersey. A lack of transportation foiled his plans. However, it was the same type of poor roads that delayed the British entrance into the fort. The path the British had to climb up the Palisades was narrow, steep and less than four feet wide. In *The Long Retreat,* Lefkowitz quotes Lieutenant Henry Stirke of the Light Infantry, who was one of the first men ashore during the siege. Stirke reported that there was a "precipice, above a half mile in length." He said that this precipice was "impassable for horses." A Hessian officer noted, "Our disembarkation appeared terrible and impracticable as we landed

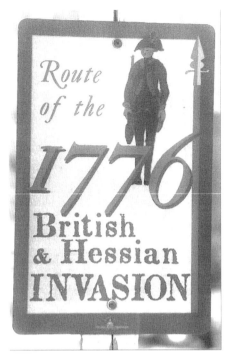

Left: Route of the 1776 British & Hessian Invasion sign commemorating the 225th anniversary in 2001, Tenafly. *Courtesy of Ira Lieblich.*

Below: Hessian Jägers and British troops during the Retreat to Victory, Tenafly, November 2001. *Courtesy of Ira Lieblich.*

at the foot of a rocky height and had to go up a very steep and narrow path...Fifty men would have sufficed to hold back the entire corps if they had only hurled stones down on us." After the British crested the Palisade cliffs, they used sheer manpower to drag cannons and other supplies down "rocky" Closter Dock Road.

Although Americans did not employ the strategy feared by the Hessian officer, they did gain additional time to make their retreat. Throughout the retreat from Fort Lee, the militia commanded an excellent local knowledge of the roads. They began their retreat by marching down Fort Lee Road. This road was specifically designed as a military road and had been created by the Continental army. Most of the troops marched north on Kings Highway, now called Grand Avenue, in Leonia. The troops met Washington at Liberty Pole in Englewood. The overall retreat was far from organized. Some panicked soldiers broke away from the main column and marched south through the English Neighborhood and the now-titled Ridgefield to Little Ferry.

After an exhausting day of retreat, the Continentals convened in Hackensack. The knowledge that the roads were so narrow that soldiers were confined to walk two abreast—and that the retreat happened so hastily that some soldiers lacked shoes—adds a level of wonder to the triumph of the getaway. Lefkowitz quotes Thomas Paine: "It is great credit to us, that, with a handful of men, we sustained an orderly retreat for near an hundred miles, brought off our ammunition, all our field-pieces, the great part of our stores, and had four rivers to pass."

The actions of the Americans and British throughout the retreat highlight differing concepts that the opposing troops held of the roads. The retreating Americans left eight pieces of artillery and four pieces

The Liberty Fife and Drum Corps performing in Leonia during the Retreat to Victory, November 2001. By the time of the Revolution, armies had adopted a system of commands given by the drum and fife that could rapidly communicate orders to whole armies at one time. *Courtesy of Ira Lieblich.*

Continental army retreating down Fort Lee Road, Leonia, during the Retreat to Victory, November 2001. *Courtesy of Barbara Marchant.*

of light artillery during the retreat to hasten their speed. The roads were full of muskets and knapsacks that the American troops deposited along the road. The British marched in formation at a leisurely pace. Perhaps they were weighed down by all they carried, and perhaps their cultural norms of marching were too engrained for them to walk the roads in any other way. Indeed, the troops certainly had differing conceptions of effective marching. In times of battle, American troops abandoned roadways to take shelter behind trees and walls. The rigid British marching lines were left with little to shoot at in skirmishes. The Americans were emboldened with a willingness to traverse more than roads. In *The Revolutionary War in the Hackensack Valley,* Adrian Leiby notes one instance in which the American army detached "two hundred of their men with orders to march east… through the fields to the edge of the Bergen Woods so that they could fix guards on the roads." Many British troops were limited to the confines of narrow and unmade roads, which hindered their marching. This is juxtaposed with the Americans who traversed the roads and in areas that surrounded the roads.

The retreat from Fort Lee is one of many examples that highlight the significance that the Revolutionary roads of Bergen County had throughout the war. As the war progressed, the British made better use of the roads in Bergen County. Loyalist information helped increase the British knowledge of the roads. Leiby related one story of a Loyalist who walked a herd of cows down Overkill Road. His presence went undetected as he walked slowly behind the cows. He walked past the Americans' picket guard unquestioned due to his disguise as a herder. After observing military positions he abandoned the cows in a nearby field and bolted to the British headquarters at New Bridge. When he arrived he was able to report American positions accurately.

When the British lacked Loyalist knowledge they relied on spies to explore and navigate the roads. A map that Major John André drew is still preserved today. This map depicts Schraalenburgh Road and other roads throughout the English Neighborhood. The creation of this road map shows the value the British placed on gaining knowledge of the roads. Although the British acquired increasing knowledge of the roads, they remained hesitant to stray too far from the roadways. On September 23, 1778, five thousand British Regulars camped along New Bridge Road. They stretched from Liberty Pole to New Bridge. Perhaps their decision to encamp spread out along the road instead of consolidating into the towns reveals a fear of straying from the main roadways.

Throughout the war, the British marched along the roadways of Bergen County to pillage through towns and stock up on supplies. One example is when the British stripped Tappan of supplies. After a successful foraging they divided into two columns to march back to their camp. One unit took Closter Road and the other marched along Schraalenburgh Road. In other instances, foraging was prevented by weather conditions. In the winter months, weather became a determining factor in the accessibility of roads. On February 10, 1779, three hundred British light horse soldiers attempted to enter Hackensack from New York in the hopes of raiding the town and procuring supplies. They were met by deep snow and unbroken roads and did not proceed further. In this case, poor road conditions prevented what could have been a detrimental attack to Hackensack.

The winter of 1779 became so cold that the North (Hudson) River froze over. Some reports indicate that there was eleven feet of ice on the river. The British feared the Americans would cross the ice and attack New York City. Troops were afforded natural bridges in lieu of the steel crossing that would be constructed many years later. However, an attack was never made. The frozen Hudson is an example of naturally created infrastructure. There were other times during the war when altering road infrastructure would became a part of military strategy. When the Americans retreated through Hackensack, they left New Bridge intact. However, after they successfully crossed the Passaic River they destroyed the bridge over the Passaic to limit British access.

The Americans' use of roads in Bergen County reveals what might be called a faith for the local roads. In a letter that General Nathanael Greene wrote about moving supplies from Fort Lee, he professed higher trust in roads than water. In *The Revolutionary War in the Hackensack Valley*, Leiby quotes a letter from Greene, who wrote, "The powder and fixed ammunition I have sent off first by land, as it is an article too valuable to trust upon the water." At a time when many people used water as their primary choice of transport, Greene had a deeper trust in the roads. He used these roads to transport critical military supplies. Although roads were trusted by the Americans, roads remained a far from perfect way of travel for the army. Leiby also cites a letter that Lee wrote to Washington about a march in New Jersey. General Charles Lee described a march of thirty miles "through mountains, swamps and deep morasses…on a route admissible of interception at several points by a march of two, three or four miles." The possibility for interception and skirmishes left some of the American troops fearful to march the roads of Bergen County.

Throughout the Revolution, the roads of Bergen County were frequently traversed by both armies for their strategic benefit. In the 226 years since the Revolution ended, the roads of Bergen County have evolved to become what we know them today. Interestingly enough, local road responsibilities are still modeled after the British system that existed during the Revolution. Certain municipal roads continue to be governed by state, county and local jurisdictions. Although some aspects of the Revolutionary roads remain alive today, others have begun to fade away.

On the website of the Historic Roads Organization, the organization comments on the process of forgetting historically significant roads. They remark, "Across the United States, historic roads are being lost through demolition, neglect and poor management. Sometimes this is due to policy, sometimes external pressures and sometimes simply ignorance. These losses can be swift and devastating or slow and incremental—hardly noticed until it is too late." It is probable that some roads and paths used in Bergen County during the Revolution will remain undiscovered. Nature has worked to reclaim farm roads of the past. Development has assisted in erasing Revolutionary roads.

Historic marker on Kinderkamack Road, Emerson. *Courtesy of Ira Lieblich.*

Historic marker on Franklin Avenue, Franklin Lakes. *Courtesy of Ira Lieblich.*

However, other roads that were significant during the Revolution remain prominent today. In 1960 the Bergen County Historical Society began the Historic Sites Marker Program to assist in retelling the past histories of Bergen County. In the years since the program's inception, over one hundred markers have been placed on historically significant sites, including roads and avenues. They include Closter Dock Road, Huyler's Landing Road, Kinderkamack, Franklin Avenue, Schraalenburgh Road, Historic Glen Avenue and more. The BCHS explains that these markers "are designed to educate the general public with a 'mini-history lesson' for a particular site or area and are also helpful in generating interest in historic preservation." When we are traveling down the roads of Bergen County, these markers help to remind us of the people traveling on the roads before us. These markers inform pedestrians and drivers of what moment of history unfolded on the same streets that remain in use today.

When looking back 226 years ago at the strategic uses of Bergen County roads during the Revolution, striking similarities and apparent differences come to light. Drivers continue to have faith that the roads they tread on will bring them to their destination. Maps remain a critical aspect of bringing us efficiently to our destination. Residents in Bergen County supplied troops with local knowledge of Bergen County highways throughout the duration of the American Revolution. Local knowledge

Left: Historic marker on Rockleigh Road, Rockleigh. *Courtesy of Ira Lieblich.*

Below: Historic marker at Washington Spring, Van Saun Park, Paramus. *Courtesy of Ira Lieblich.*

is still relied on today when we venture into a new town. When heading down a small street with which we are unfamiliar, we might likely find ourselves asking someone for directions. The Continentals used the roads of Bergen County strategically, which worked to their military benefit. One such strategic choice was to avoid marching in the rigid formations that the British were known to keep. Even today, Americans continue to use the roads in a different way than the English since we drive on the right-hand side of the road and they on the left.

Thankfully, road conditions have improved significantly since the Revolution. The automobile brings us to our destination faster than the troops of the Revolution could ever move. Sarah Comstock warns us that our hastening speed comes with a price. In 1929, twenty-one years after the creation of the Model T, Comstock wrote that "ninety-nine hundredths of the motorists who whirr along the west shore of the Hudson never guess that they are passing close to many an old road... which played its part in the freeing of our nation." At the time Comstock wrote her book *Roads to the Revolution*, the BCHS Historic Sites Marker Program was years from existence.

Surely the blue markers help us to better understand the historically significant past of Bergen County. But when we bicycle on Rockleigh Road or drive on Howland Avenue, do we see the fervor and faith that people did so many years before us? During the war, the Americans' faith in Bergen County roads was a necessary component of their success. Now, does the calmness that our cars lull us into on a smooth, local road cause us to forget the past? In 1929 Comstock informed us that throughout Bergen County, "hidden here and there, is some tale of our history well worth the tracing to anyone who will do what the most of motorists would rather perish than do—namely, pause."

Benjamin Rubin, a Tenafly native, studies urban planning at Pitzer College in California. He has held a lifelong interest in the American Revolution and was a child reenactor for Revolutionary War events in the local area for many years.

BURDETT'S LANDING

DOUGLAS E. HALL

In every story throughout history, there are locations that are of critical importance. They may simply be a crossroads, a harbor or a landing place along a river that gave particularly easy access to an area inland. Such a New Jersey location played a critical role in the American Revolution. That place was Burdett's Landing in what is now a settlement in Edgewater known as the Edgewater Colony.

Burdett's Landing was highly valued because of the topography of the area, a small cove at, according to Arthur G. Adams in *Hudson River Guidebook*, "the bottom of a clove [i.e., ravine] giving easy access to the top of the Palisades and at the outlet of a small watercourse known as Dead Brook."

The landing is named for Etienne Burdett or Bourdette, as it was originally spelled, a French Huguenot, who had fled to the New World to escape religious persecution and became the first permanent European settler in Edgewater. In the *History of Bergen County, NJ*, written in 1900 by James M. Van Walen, it is noted that in the mid-1700s, the land that would become Burdett's Landing was owned by a freed slave, who had received it in exchange for his shoring up of the road to the top of the bluff with several hundred yards of retaining wall.

Burdett first settled in Manhattan, later buying several hundred acres on the shore of the Hudson River near the southern part of what today is Fort Lee. In 1758, he and his family established a ferry service to the eastern shore of the Hudson River. During the American Revolution, the ferry proved important to the American cause prior to and during the Battle of Fort Washington in 1776 in what is now the Washington Heights section of Manhattan.

Burdett's Landing on the Hudson River, by John George Browne. *Courtesy of Douglas E. Hall.*

Burdett also established a trading post and built his home, a gambrel-roofed structure in a forest clearing at the foot of the gorge, where it stood until 1899. A road connecting the ferry landing to the top of the Palisades later became known as Hackensack Turnpike. This route is currently known as River Road in Edgewater and Hudson Terrace in Fort Lee, which connects with Main Street in Fort Lee, becoming Fort Lee Road in Leonia, DeGraw Avenue in Teaneck, and West Main Street in Bogota before finally reaching the Hackensack River and the town of Hackensack.

Originally, Burdett's Ferry was used for the transportation of goods and passengers on a type of sailing boat called a periougas. The ferry was one of the major connecting points for the farmers who brought their produce from the inland farms of New Jersey to New York City.

During the American Revolution, Peter Burdett (1735–1826), Etienne's brother, was an ardent Patriot and operated the ferry for the Continental army as a supply line and communications network. Local lore claims his wife cooked flapjacks for General Washington and his staff officers when they were in the area of the Burdett ferry; they frequently traveled from Fort Washington across the Hudson River on the ferry and then rode or walked to Fort Lee in the town that now bears the name of that fortification. This was prior to the fall of Fort Washington in New York to the British. The importance of Burdett's Landing during the Revolution and the report of Mrs. Burdett cooking for General Washington and his staff have been passed down from a grandson of Peter Burdett, J. Fletcher Burdett, and a resident of Fort Lee in 1900.

Burdett's ferry had the distinction of being involved in two military engagements in 1776 during the siege of Fort Washington. The first occurred on August 17, 1776, and the second on October 27, 1776. Both battles were against the British ships HMS *Rose* and HMS *Phoenix*, both of which sustained damage. The barbette battery on the Fort Lee bluffs opened fire and two eighteen-pounders brought down to the ferry landing from Fort Lee repeatedly punctured the hulls and partially disabled one of the ships. Adams notes in his *Hudson River Guidebook* that General Nathanael Greene wrote, "Had the tide been flood one half-hour longer, we should have sunk her."

The fortifications successfully engaged other British frigates and ships of war, and many important campaigns were won due to the armaments mounted on the Edgewater shore.

A time-worn historic marker in the Edgewater Colony states,

> *In the time of the Revolution, the road turned here* [reference is to River Road near Annette Place where marker was originally placed, which has since moved to Annette near the Edgewater Colony clubhouse] *and followed the brook to Peter Burdett's ferry, the important Hudson River approach to General Nathaniel Green's encampment at Fort Lee, on the hill, and the connecting link with the American forces on the opposite shore. South of the brook stood the Burdett homestead,* [General George] *Washington's local headquarters. Washington, Greene,* [General Israel] *Putnam and others, crossed frequently here, dispatch-bearers arrived and departed, troops and military stores were landed at the wharf. A memorial near the river recalls the engagements of Aug. 18, Oct. 8, 9, and 27, 1776, between General* [Hugh] *Mercer's shore battery of 18-pounders and certain British ships-of-war.*

The marker states that it was "prepared for the (borough) mayor and council by the Edgewater Committee of Historic sites, Edgewater, New Jersey, July 4, 1952."

In the days before the Battle of Fort Washington on November 16, 1776, there were many communications between the fort in New York and the fort in New Jersey. On the west side of the Hudson River, Burdett's Landing played a critical part. On the night before the British stormed Fort

HUDSON RIVER, BERGEN C

British Warships on the Hudson. Illustration by permission of Gray's Watercolors, grayswatercolors@ rcn.com.

Washington in New York, General Washington met with his senior officers in a boat in the middle of the Hudson River.

The last time the ferry was used during the conflict was to transport Captain John Gooch across the Hudson to deliver a letter from General Washington to Colonel Robert Magaw, commanding officer of the beleaguered Fort Washington. Unfortunately, the letter was never delivered due to the heat of the battle and the fort being surrounded by British troops advancing from the south and the Hessians from the north. Gooch barely made it back to the boat that had transported him across the river. He returned safely to Fort Lee to report his unsuccessful trip to General Washington. Fort Lee was not safe for long and fell four days after the fall of Fort Washington.

After a year of retreats from Brooklyn to New York, across the Hudson River and down through New Jersey to Pennsylvania, the tide was finally turned on the day after Christmas 1776, when Washington and about 2,500 Continental soldiers crossed the ice-clogged Delaware River from Pennsylvania, surprising Hessian mercenaries in the British service encamped at Trenton. The war was far from over, and there would be more defeats for the Continental army, but they were on the road to victory that would lead to the surrender of the British under General Charles Cornwallis at Yorktown in 1781 and an eventual end of the war with victory for the Americans in 1783.

After the war, the new country of the United States got about the business of building a nation, and Burdett's Landing and ferry service returned to transporting goods and passengers across the Hudson River. By the 1800s, Edgewater and Fort Lee began to experience a growth in tourism. Opulent hotels were built near Burdett's Landing, and the new steamboats on the river made regular stops at Burdett's, dropping off and picking up passengers who stayed at the new hotels.

In the 1860s, the Fort Lee Park Hotel stood on a twenty-six-acre parcel. The hotel was popular with many New Yorkers, offering entertainment, gambling and an array of sports. The hotel was completely destroyed by fire in 1914, and the site became a homestead for many poor working-class families, according to Adams.

As industry developed in the southern part of Edgewater toward the end of the nineteenth century and into the twentieth century, tourism faded, hurried to its demise by a devastating fire at one of the major hotels. The landing was abandoned as other ferry lines were developed in other locations on the Hudson River. Left to time and the elements, it rotted away until only a few pilings were left sticking out of the river. The last of these disappeared in the swift tide of the river until today one can see no evidence that Burdett's Landing ever existed.

———•———

Douglas E. Hall is currently editor of two weekly newspapers and former editor/ publisher/owner of a nationally distributed newsletter. He is also the author of Images of America: Edgewater. *He is chair of the Edgewater Cultural and Historical Committee and was the chairman of the Mayor's Advisory Committee on Ferries.*

THE MYSTERIOUS DEATH OF
BRIGADIER GENERAL ENOCH POOR

RICHARD BURNON

Was Brigadier General Enoch Poor, a Revolutionary War hero and one of General George Washington's favorite officers, killed in a secret duel with one of his subordinate officers or did he die of typhoid fever (or putrid fever, as it was known then) on September 8, 1780, as a surgeon in the Continental army stated?

For over two hundred years, General Poor's death remained a closely guarded secret. Then, an obscure book in the New York Public Library revealed the true facts behind the death of General Poor, who is buried in the graveyard of the First Reformed Church in Hackensack. The book, *Poor Family Gatherings, 1881–1896*, is believed to be the only one of its kind on the general and his descendants.

The account of the duel was related by Major Benjamin Perley Poore, a descendant of General Poor, during a family reunion on September 10, 1884, at Andover, Massachusetts, General Poor's hometown.

According to Major Poore's account, General Poor was killed in a secret duel with a Major John Porter Jr. on September 8, 1780. The general was forty-four years old.

General Poor was in command of a brigade of light infantry in the division led by the Marquis de Lafayette. The brigade was intended to be a model in drill and discipline.

Major Porter, according to the book, was one of General Poor's subordinate officers. During a forced march near Oradell on September 7, 1780, Major Porter's men halted beneath some trees to rest, since the day was extremely hot. The men were tired, hungry and thirsty. Shortly thereafter, General Poor rode up and commanded Porter to call up his men and continue on the

Statue of General Enoch Poor and the Church-on-the-Green (First Reformed Church), Hackensack. *Courtesy of Ira Lieblich.*

Historic marker at Soldier Hill, Kinderkamack Road, Oradell. *Courtesy of Ira Lieblich.*

march. Major Porter repeated the order, but not a man in his section moved. General Poor rode up a second time and repeated his order.

The general then proceeded to criticize Major Porter in front of his men. Porter regarded the remarks as personally offensive and told Poor that if their military ranks were equal, Porter would challenge the general to a duel. General Poor then waived his privileges as the commanding officer. Porter obtained the services of a friend as a second. The challenge was sent and accepted by General Poor.

At daybreak on September 8, 1780, the duel was fought. The referee arranged that the men should stand back-to-back with loaded pistols. When the referee uttered the word "march," the two men moved five paces forward, halted and fired their pistols over their left shoulders. After the pistols were fired, the two men were supposed to turn toward each other and finish the duel with swords. In this case, Major Porter's shot mortally wounded General Poor. Porter, who wasn't wounded, drew his sword, but was stopped by his second. Porter then left the field and the dying general.

Dueling during the Revolutionary War was frowned upon and even considered a court-martial offense. A rumor filtered through the camp indicating that the general had been killed in a duel with a French officer.

Two days after the secret duel, General Poor was buried with full military honors, with General George Washington, the Marquis de Lafayette and other senior American military officers in attendance. Washington wrote to Congress of Poor's death, saying in part, "He was an officer of distinguished merit, one who as a citizen and soldier had every claim to the esteem and regard of his country." Congress ordered the letter printed for the public, as an indication of respect for Enoch Poor.

Major Porter, who had once studied to be a minister, was relieved of his command soon after the duel and returned with Lafayette to France at the end of the war in 1783. He became a successful wine merchant in Calais and died in 1818 at the age of seventy-six.

Tablet in Church-on-the-Green cemetery in honor of General Enoch Poor, Hackensack. *Courtesy of Ira Lieblich.*

In 1824, when Lafayette revisited General Poor's grave, he turned away and exclaimed, "Ah, That was one of my Generals."

Poor was born June 21, 1736, in Andover, Massachusetts, and raised there. His father, Thomas Poor, had been part of the 1745 expedition that captured Louisburg, Nova Scotia, during King George's War. In 1755 young Poor enlisted as a private in one of the Massachusetts units raised to accompany Jeffrey Amherst's expedition to retake Louisburg during the French and Indian War. His unit enforced the expulsion of the Acadians. After the war, he came home to Andover, but only briefly. Poor eloped with Martha Osgood, and the newlyweds settled in Exeter, New Hampshire.

Poor supported the separatists as early as the Stamp Act protests in 1765. He served on various committees for the town throughout the period of rising rebellion. In 1775 he was twice elected to the Provincial Assembly. When the Battle of Lexington caused the assembly to call for three regiments of militia, Poor became the colonel of the Second New Hampshire Regiment.

While the other regiments under Colonels John Stark and James Reed were sent to Boston, the Second was stationed at Portsmouth and Exeter. After the Battle of Bunker Hill, they were also sent to Boston, arriving on June 25, 1775. In the summer of 1775, the unit was absorbed into the Continental army. They were soon ordered into the Northern Department and went with General Richard Montgomery's invasion of Canada.

After the Canadian disaster, Poor led the survivors of his regiment in early 1776 back to Fort Ticonderoga. After refitting and recruiting, the unit was renamed as the Eighth Continental Regiment and joined Washington's main army in December 1776, near Morristown, New Jersey.

The Continental Congress named Poor a brigadier general on February 21, 1777. That spring, his brigade of three New Hampshire (First, Second and Third) and two New York (Second and Fourth) regiments was sent back to Fort Ticonderoga. He withdrew with the rest of Arthur St. Clair's force on July 5, 1777. Moving south, they joined General Horatio Gates before the Battle of Saratoga, and Poor's brigade was expanded with two regiments of Connecticut militia (Cook's and Latimer's).

In the first engagement of Saratoga, the Battle of Freeman's Farm, Poor's brigade was the first to come to the aid of Daniel Morgan's attack. Poor held the American left flank, extending into the woods and even wrapping around the British position. They performed well, keeping General Simon Fraser's regulars engaged, while American General Benedict Arnold led attacks on the central column.

In the second engagement, the Battle of Bemis Heights, Poor's brigade was in General Benjamin Lincoln's division on the left (western) end of the American line. They were closest to the center of the advancing British, so they came under fire from the Grenadier Battalion of the British center. The fire was ineffective, so the British Major John Dyke Acland led the grenadiers in a bayonet charge. Poor held fire until they came very near, then opened up with the massed fire of his 1,400 men. These were the first American shots in the battle. The charge was completely broken, and Acland himself fell wounded. With this collapse of Burgoyne's center, the Americans captured the wounded Acland and Major Williams, along with the column's artillery. Poor then turned to his left and gave support to Ebenezer Learned and Morgan's men.

Poor's brigade again spent the winter with the main army, this time at Valley Forge. He led the last maneuvers in the Battle of Monmouth on June 28, 1778. Poor accompanied the Sullivan expedition in 1779, leading a brigade in the victory at Newton. Afterward, Poor was assigned to Lafayette's division and mainly saw garrison duty in New Jersey.

The general's statue now stands at the triangular intersection of Moore and Court Streets in Hackensack. Very few residents and visitors stop to look at the Revolutionary War hero's features, pockmarked by the elements, age and lack of maintenance. The general's sword and the spur on his left boot have long since been snapped off by pranksters. A chalk-green mold is slowly enveloping the general's copper composition. The statue was dedicated in the general's memory to the City of Hackensack in 1904 by the New Jersey Society of the Sons of the American Revolution. Hackensack acknowledged General Poor on the 225th anniversary of his death in 2005.

Bergen County historians are split in their opinions about the cause of General Poor's death. Some feel that the account of the general's death was accurately described in *Military Journal of the American Revolution*, written by James Thacher, MD. Thacher was a surgeon in the Continental army and wrote an elaborate account of General Poor's military funeral.

Others feel that the Poor-Porter duel could have taken place in secret, and that Washington could have ordered Thacher to cover up the death of General Poor. Duelists were subject to court-martial if caught.

Thacher's *Military Journal* is regarded as a semi-official publication. But historians agree that it could be in error.

There is James Porter, a descendant of Major Porter and a retired New York advertising executive, who claims that General Poor was a scoundrel, not a hero. Porter, a history buff, claims to have discovered a packet of letters in an old chest that were purportedly written by Major Porter to his wife, Abigail, from 1777 to 1780. In one of the letters, Major Porter wrote that General Poor's "uninspired leadership" during the Battle of Monmouth Courthouse in June 1778 almost cost the Continental army its victory over the British.

In another letter, dated June 30, 1778, Major Porter cited two instances in which he personally saved the general's life. The letter read in part, "When I saw his horse shot from under him (Poor), I jumped off my horse and helped him off the ground. Poor's face was pale from the experience. Both of us rode back into camp on my horse." In another instance, Major Porter claims he shot a British soldier who was about to shoot General Poor in the back.

The Porter descendant said that instead of showing his gratitude, General Poor constantly belittled the major in front of the latter's men. He said General Poor also refused to endorse a promotion to colonel for the major. Mr. Porter feels that historians should set the record straight about General Poor and see him for what he felt he was: a mediocre military leader and a scoundrel to boot. Obviously, Colonel Porter would bear a grudge against General Poor and would not write of him in good terms.

Of course, there are those who believe that General Poor did die of illness. Poor's adjutant, Major Jeremiah Fogg, gave a deposition in 1781 and claimed that the general's cause of death was fever.

What is the truth concerning the circumstances of General Poor's death? If you speak with ten historians, you may come up with ten different answers. We may never know the full truth, except that some of Poor's men spoke glowingly of him while others did not.

Richard Burnon

Richard Burnon has been a writer for five decades. He holds a BA in journalism from Rutgers, the State University of New Jersey. His background includes newspaper reporter, trade magazine editor and corporate and nonprofit public relations. In addition, he has written numerous historical articles and press releases over the years for college papers and newspapers, particularly biographical sketches of General Enoch Poor, musical icons Buddy Holly and Patsy Cline, sharpshooter Annie Oakley, 1872 presidential candidate Victoria Woodhull, Huey Long, Abigail Adams, one-armed World War II ballplayer Pete Gray and many others.

William J. Boerner, drummer. *Courtesy of Diane Boerner-Lettieri.*

BIBLIOGRAPHY

Beardslee, John W., III. "The Reformed Church and the American Revolution." In *Piety and Patriotism: Bicentennial Studies of the Reformed Church in America, 1776–1976*, edited by James W. Van Hoeven. Grand Rapids, MI: The General Synod of the Reformed Church in America, 1976.

"Bergen County Patriots." *Bergen County History: Annual of the Bergen County Historical Society*. River Edge, NJ: Bergen County Historical Society, 1976.

Bill, Alfred Hoyt. *New Jersey and the Revolutionary War*. Princeton, NJ: D. Van Nostrand Company, Inc., 1964.

Burroughs, Edwin G. *Forgotten Patriots: The Untold Story of American Prisoners During the Revolutionary War*. New York: Basic Books, 2008.

Chartrand, René. *American War of Independence Commanders*. Oxford, Great Britain: Osprey Publishing, 2003.

Commager, Henry Steele, and Richard B. Morris, eds. *The Spirit of Seventy-Six: The Story of the American Revolution as told by Participants*. New York: DaCapo Press, 1995.

Corwin, Charles E., ed. *A Manual of the Reformed Church in America, 1628–1922*. 5th ed. New York: Board of the Publication of the Reformed Church in America, 1922.

Corwin, E.T., ed. *Ecclesiastical Records of the State of New York*. 7 vols. Albany: State of New York, 1901–16.

De Jong, Gerald F. *The Dutch Reformed Church in the American Colonies*. Grand Rapids, MI: Wm. B. Eerdmans Publishing Company, 1978.

Demarest, Voorhis D., ed. *The Demarest Family*. New York: Westview Press, 1964.

DiIonno, Mark. *A Guide to New Jersey's Revolutionary War Trail*. Camden, NJ: Rutgers University Press, 2000.

Ellis, Joseph J. *His Excellency George Washington*. New York: Alfred A. Knopf, 2004.

Ewald, Captain Johann. *Diary of the American War, A Hessian Journal*. Translated and edited by Joseph Tustin. New Haven, CT: Yale University Press, 1979.

Fabend, Firth Haring. *A Dutch Family in the Middle Colonies, 1660–1800*. New Brunswick, NJ: Rutgers University Press, 1991.

———. *Land So Fair*. Lincoln, NE: iUniverse, 2008.

Fischer, David Hackett. *Washington's Crossing*. New York: Oxford University Press, 2004.

"Fort Lee: The Post at Burdett's Ferry." *Bergen County History: Annual of the Bergen County Historical Society*. River Edge, NJ: Bergen County Historical Society, 1975.

Gerlach, Larry R., ed. *New Jersey in the American Revolution, 1763–1783: A Documentary History*. Trenton: New Jersey Historical Commission, 1975.

Glover, T.N. *The Retreat Across Bergen County*. N.p.: Bergen County Historical Society, 1905.

Greene, Jerome A. *The Guns of Independence: The Siege of Yorktown, 1781*. New York: Savas Beatie, 2005

Greene, Nathanael. *The Papers of Nathanael Greene*. Chapel Hill: University of North Carolina/Rhode Island Historical Society, 1976.

Harvey, Robert. *A Few Bloody Noses: The American Revolutionary War*. London: Constable & Robinson, 2004.

Headley, Hon. J.T. *The Illustrated Life of Washington*. New York: G.&F. Bill, 1860.

Heusser, Albert H. *George Washington's Map Maker: A Biography of Robert Erskine*. New Brunswick, NJ: Rutgers University Press, 1966.

Honeyman, A. Van Doren. *Documents Relating to the Colonial History of the State of New Jersey*. Vol. 21. Somerville, NJ: The Unionist-Gazette Association, 1923.

Humphrey, David C. *From King's College to Columbia, 1746–1800*. New York: Columbia University Press, 1976.

Karels, Carol, ed. *The Revolutionary War in Bergen County: The Times That Tried Men's Souls*. Charleston, SC: The History Press, 2007.

Lee, Francis B., William Nelson, Austin Scott and William S. Stryker, eds. *Documents Relating to the Colonial History of the State of New Jersey*. Second Series, Volumes I–V. Trenton: (various), 1901, 1903, 1906, 1914, 1917.

Lefkowitz, Arthur S. *George Washington's Indispensable Men The 32 Aides-de-Camp Who Helped Win American Independence.* Mechanicsburg, PA: Stackpole Books, 2003.

———. *The Long Retreat: The Calamitous American Defense of New Jersey, 1776.* Metuchen, NJ: Upland Press, 1998.

Leiby, Adrian C. *The Early Dutch and Swedish Settlers of New Jersey.* Princeton, NJ: D. Van Nostrand Co., Inc., 1964.

———. *The Revolutionary War in the Hackensack Valley: The Jersey Dutch and the Neutral Ground 1775–1783.* 1962. New Brunswick, NJ: Rutgers University Press, 1992.

Lengel, Edward G. *This Glorious Struggle: George Washington's Revolutionary War Letters.* New York: HarperCollins Publishers, 2007.

Lorant, Stefan. "The Founding Father: George Washington." *The Keynoter: The Journal of the American Political Items Collectors* (Spring/Summer 2006).

Lossing, Benjamin. *Pictorial Field-Book of the Revolution.* 2 vols. New York: Harper Brothers, 1850.

Lydekker, John Wolfe. "The Rev. Gerrit (Gerard) Lydecker, 1729–1794." *Historical Magazine,* 1944.

"Major Aldington." *Bergen County History: The Annual of the Bergen County Historical Society.* River Edge, NJ: Bergen County Historical Society, 1970.

Marston, David. *The American Revolution, 1774–1783.* Oxford, Great Britain: Osprey Publishing, 2002.

Martin, Joseph Plumb. *Private Yankee Doodle.* Edited by George E. Scheer. New York: Eastern Acorn Press, 1995.

McCullough, David. *1776.* New York: Simon and Schuster, 2005

Romeyn, Rev. Theodore B. *Historical Discourse Delivered on Occasion of the Re-Opening and Dedication of the First Reformed (Dutch) Church at Hackensack, N.J. May 2, 1869.* New York: Board of Publication, R.C.A., 1870.

Rosenfeld, Ross. "The Fox Bares His Fangs." *Great Battles: Turning Points in the American Revolution.* Leesburg, VA: Primedia Enthusiast Group, 2005.

Schecter, Barnet. *The Battle for New York: The City at the Heart of the American Revolution.* New York: Walker & Company, 2002.

Smith, David. *New York, 1776.* Oxford, Great Britain: Osprey Publishing, 2008.

Sparks, Jared. *The Writings of George Washington (being his Correspondence, Addresses, Messages, and other Papers, official and private, Part Second.* Boston: Russell, Odiorne, and Metcalf, and Hilliard, Gray, and Co., 1834.

Spring, John. *The 1776 British Landing at Closter.* River Edge, NJ: Bergen County Historical Society, 1975.

Stryker-Rodda, Kenn. *Revolutionary Census of New Jersey*, Cottonport, LA: Polyanthos, 1972

Thacher, James. *Military Journal of the American Revolution.* Hartford, CT: Hurlbut, Williams & Co., 1862.

Thompson, Henry P. *History of the Reformed Church, at Readington, N.J., 1719–1881.* New York: Board of Publication of the Reformed Church of America, 1882.

Manuscripts

Adjutant General's Office, Loyalist Manuscripts. New Jersey State Archives.

Department of Defense. Military Records, Revolutionary War, Revolutionary Manuscripts Numbered. New Jersey State Archives, Washington, D.C.

Headquarters Papers of the British army in America. National Archives of the United Kingdom.

Lidgerwood Collection of Hessian Transcripts. Morristown National Historical Park.

"Return of the Killed, Wounded & Missing at the attack of the Rebel Troops at Paramus in Jersey, the 23rd March 1780." William L. Clements Library, University of Michigan, Ann Arbor.

Spencer, George, to John G. Simcoe, undated (with enclosure, map of Hopper's Town), John Graves Simcoe Papers 1774–1824, William L. Clements Library, University of Michigan.

Washington, George. Papers. September–December 1776. Library of Congress, Washington, D.C.

———. Series 4, General Correspondence. March 6, 1780–April 24, 1780. Library of Congress, Washington, D.C.

Newspapers

Bee and Paterson Advertiser

Bergen County Democrat

Bergen County Journal (Hackensack)

Hester, Tom. *Star Ledger, Center of the Storm, NJ and American Revolution.* Edited by Len Meliswigo, Kean University, 2001.

New Jersey Citizen

New Jersey Gazette (Trenton)
New Jersey Journal
New-York Gazette and the Weekly Mercury
Royal Gazette (New York)

Unpublished Sources

Bergen County Deed Book C, D, J8
Bergen County Mortgage Book A

Index

INDEX

INDEX

Visit us at
www.historypress.net